Hostile Hallways

Bullying, Teasing, and Sexual Harassment in School

Commissioned by

AAUW EDUCATIONAL FOUNDATION

Researched by Harris Interactive
111 Fifth Avenue, New York, NY 10003, 212/539-9600, www.harrisinteractive.com
Project Directors: Anne Axelrod, Ph.D., Senior Vice President, and Dana Markow, Ph.D., Project Manager

Published by the American Association of University Women Educational Foundation
1111 Sixteenth St. N.W.
Washington, DC 20036
202/728-7602
Fax: 202/463-7169
TDD: 202/785-7777
foundation@aauw.org
www.aauw.org

First printing: May 2001
Layout and design: Julie A. Hamilton
Editor: Jodi Lipson
Cover photo: Nicholas E. Waring

Library of Congress Catalog Card Number: 2001089696
ISBN 1-879922-28-2

Printed on
recycled paper

308/01 05/01 9M

Table of Contents

Foreword
From AAUW

I n investigating the events that led up to the unfortunate shootings at Columbine and other schools, the police revealed several similar conditions.

For the AAUW Educational Foundation, one similarity stood out: The students who fired the guns were picked on. Bullied. Teased. Harassed.

Since its first study in 1881 debunking the myth that higher education jeopardized women's health, the American Association of University Women has been on the cutting edge of research affecting women, girls, and education. *Hostile Hallways: Bullying, Teasing, and Sexual Harassment in School,* conducted in our 120th year, again looks closely at a modern-day problem that deeply affects students' learning.

Sexual harassment—and all the bullying, teasing, and touching it entails—is pervasive: Four out of every five students personally experience it. While many students say harassment is no big deal—just part of school life—names do hurt: "a kid called me a fag"; "sexual name calling"; "simple verbal assault"; "girls spreading rumors about me." Physical acts hurt, too: "someone forced my clothes off"; "a guy grabbed my butt"; "I saw a boy who put his hands down a girl's shirt and then down her pants but she could do nothing about it because he was cool." These are some of the ways that students describe harassment in their schools. And whether words or actions, harassment upsets students and affects their everyday school lives. They begin avoiding certain routes, changing their seats, being afraid.

Armed with the updated information in this report, parents, educators, activists, and policy-makers can better address problems before they become crises. While machines can detect guns in book bags, we all need to work together—and with our children—to recognize and deal with bullying, teasing, and harassment before they escalate to one more Columbine.

Sharon Schuster

Sharon Schuster
President
AAUW Educational Foundation

Introduction

This report was conducted by Harris Interactive for the American Association of University Women Educational Foundation. It revisits issues originally researched in *Hostile Hallways: The AAUW Survey on Sexual Harassment in America's Schools,* also conducted by Harris (then Louis Harris and Associates), in 1993. This new study investigates secondary school students' experiences of sexual harassment—and all the bullying, teasing, and touching it entails—and compares those with the situation eight years ago. Topics in this survey include students' knowledge and awareness of sexual harassment, personal experiences with sexual harassment in their school lives, and the emotional and behavioral impact of these experiences.

Survey Method

For this study, Harris interviewed a nationally representative sample of 2,064 public school students in eighth through 11th grades (compared to 1,632 in 1993). Using self-administered questionnaires, 1,559 students were surveyed during an English class and 505 students were surveyed online. School interviews averaged 38 minutes and online interviews averaged 15 minutes. Interviews were conducted between Sept. 7 and Nov. 22, 2000. A detailed methodology appears in the appendix. The survey questionnaire is available through Harris Interactive (www.harrisinteractive.com).

Reading the Tables and Graphs

An asterisk (*) in a figure signals a value of less than one-half (0.5) percent. A dash (-) represents a value of zero. Percentages may not always add up to 100 percent because of computer rounding or multiple answers from respondents. Calculations of responses discussed in the text are based on raw numbers and not percentages, so these calculations may differ slightly from calculations based on percentages in the figures.

The base (N) for each question is the total number of respondents answering that question. In some cases—typically true when questions were asked of subgroups—results may be based on small sample sizes. Caution should be used in drawing any conclusions from the results based on these small samples. Percentages depicted in a figure may not add up to 100 percent because some answer categories may be excluded from the figure.

Project Responsibility and Acknowledgments

The Harris team responsible for the design and analysis of the survey included Anne Axelrod, senior vice president, and Dana Markow, project manager. Harris Interactive was responsible for final determination of the survey topics, question wording, collection of data, analysis, and interpretation.

Public Release of Survey Findings

All Harris Interactive surveys are designed to comply with the code and standards of the Council of American Survey Research Organizations and the code of the National Council of Public Polls. The complete report, with the survey instrument and total responses to each question, is available through Harris Interactive.

Executive Summary and Major Findings

Eight years ago, the AAUW Educational Foundation commissioned Louis Harris & Associates (now Harris Interactive) to conduct the first nationally representative survey on sexual harassment in public school. The original *Hostile Hallways: The AAUW Survey on Sexual Harassment in America's Schools* (1993) revealed the widespread occurrence of sexual harassment and the accompanying bullying and teasing in students' school lives and explored the impact that the harassment had on the educational environment and learning experience. This current survey, also by Harris, revisits these issues:

■ Do students view sexual harassment as a large problem in their school?

■ Are students aware that their schools have a policy or distribute literature on sexual harassment?

■ How often do students experience sexual harassment in their school lives?

■ How do boys and girls differ in their experience of school sexual harassment?

■ What role does the type or frequency of sexual harassment have on students' experiences?

■ What are the emotional and behavioral consequences of sexual harassment?

■ What changes concerning these issues have occurred since 1993?

Students' answers were analyzed, where possible, to identify any difference by gender, race/ethnicity (white, black, or Hispanic), grade level (eighth and ninth or 10th and 11th), and area of school (urban or suburban/rural).

Harassment in Schools

As in 1993, today nearly all students say they know what sexual harassment is. When asked to provide their own definitions, students mention physical and nonphysical behaviors: touch, words, looks, and gestures.

For the purposes of this survey, students were given the following definition of sexual harassment:

Sexual harassment is **unwanted** and **unwelcome** sexual behavior that interferes with your life. Sexual harassment is **not** behaviors that you **like** or **want** (for example **wanted** kissing, touching, or flirting).

EXAMPLES OF HARASSMENT

❖ Made sexual comments, jokes, gestures, or looks

❖ Showed, gave, or left you sexual pictures, photographs, illustrations, messages, or notes

❖ Wrote sexual messages/graffiti about you on bathroom walls, in locker rooms, etc.

❖ Spread sexual rumors about you

❖ Said you were gay or lesbian

❖ Spied on you as you dressed or showered at school

❖ Flashed or "mooned" you

❖ Touched, grabbed, or pinched you in a sexual way

❖ Intentionally brushed up against you in a sexual way

❖ Pulled at your clothing in a sexual way

❖ Pulled off or down your clothing

❖ Blocked your way or cornered you in a sexual way

❖ Forced you to kiss him/her

❖ Forced you to do something sexual other than kissing

Students were also given 14 examples of harassment. Half the examples involve physical contact, while half do not.

One way to categorize these examples is on a continuum, from nonphysical to physical. Students say the most upsetting acts, however, span the nonphysical and physical. About equal numbers of students—three-quarters of those surveyed—say they would be very upset if someone spread sexual rumors about them, if someone pulled off or down their clothing, or if someone called them gay or lesbian. Thus, the survey shows, some forms of speech are as upsetting as actions.

Greater Awareness of School Policies and Materials

Two findings stand out dramatically from 1993: Students today are much more likely to say their schools have a sexual harassment policy or their schools distribute literature on sexual harassment. Seven in 10 students say yes, their schools have a policy on sexual harassment, while more than one-third say yes, their schools distribute literature about this issue. Both findings represent substantial increases over 1993, when the plurality of students answered the same question with either no or I'm not sure.

Personal Experiences of School Sexual Harassment

How common is school sexual harassment? As in 1993, eight in 10 students experience some form of sexual harassment at some time during their school lives. One striking change since 1993 is the increase in the number of boys who often experience school sexual harassment.

As mentioned previously, sexual harassment encompasses a range of behaviors, both those that involve physical contact as well as those that do not. In addition, the frequency of occurrence ranges from ever experiencing to often experiencing. Is school sexual harassment as prevalent a problem when viewed by these differing definitions?

In terms of type of harassment, nonphysical is the most prevalent. Three-quarters of students ever experience this type of harassment, with more than half experiencing it often or occasionally. Physical harassment lags not far behind. The majority of students experience physical harassment at some point during their school lives, with one in three experiencing it often or occasionally. In terms of frequency, six in 10 students experience some form of sexual harassment often or occasionally, with fully one-quarter experiencing it often.

Although most students experience some form of sexual harassment during their school lives, all students' experiences are not equivalent. Girls are more likely than boys to experience nonphysical or physical harassment, and they are more likely than boys to experience it more frequently. These differing experiences may explain girls' and boys' differing views on their school environment as a whole. Girls are more likely than boys to say that they know someone who has experienced sexual harassment at school and that there is a lot of or some sexual harassment in their school.

Given the prevalence of harassment at school, how do these experiences affect students and learning? In addition to feeling upset, students report other consequences more directly tied to education. One-quarter of the students who experience harassment say they do not talk as much in class or do not want to go to school, and two in 10 found it hard to pay attention. The type of harassment plays a role in the impact. Students who experience physical harassment are more likely than those who experience nonphysical to report such behavioral and educational consequences.

Conclusions

When the original *Hostile Hallways* survey was conducted in 1993, a large majority of students had experienced sexual harassment at some point in their school lives. And for many students, this experience reverberated throughout their educational and emotional lives. Eight years later, this picture looks the same in key aspects. But students today are more likely to say their schools have a policy or distribute literature on sexual harassment.

Because of the widespread nature of sexual harassment in school life, some students report that it's not a big deal and many accept it as part of everyday life. The results of this current survey reaffirm that despite students' seemingly offhanded acceptance, experiencing sexual harassment in school life has broad consequences, both subtle and direct, on girls' and boys' education.

Major Findings

Significant numbers of students are afraid of being hurt or bothered in their school lives.

- Two in 10 students (18 percent) fear that someone will hurt or bother them at school.

- Girls and boys are almost equally likely to feel this way, and these levels do not differ substantially between urban and suburban/rural schools.

Sexual harassment is widespread in school life. While boys today are even more likely than boys in 1993 to experience sexual harassment, they are still less likely than girls to have this experience.

- Eight in 10 students (81 percent) experience some form of sexual harassment during their school lives: six in 10 (59 percent) often or occasionally and one-quarter (27 percent) often. These levels have not changed since 1993.

- Girls are more likely than boys to experience sexual harassment ever (83 percent vs. 79 percent) or often (30 percent vs. 24 percent).

- Boys today are more likely than those in 1993 to experience sexual harassment often or occasionally (56 percent vs. 49 percent) or often (24 percent vs. 18 percent).

- Three-quarters of students (76 percent) experience nonphysical sexual harassment at some point in their school lives, more than half (54 percent) often or occasionally.

- Six in 10 students (58 percent) experience physical sexual harassment at some point in their school lives, one-third (32 percent) often or occasionally.

- One-third (32 percent) of students are afraid of being sexually harassed. Girls are more than twice as likely as boys to feel this way (44 percent vs. 20 percent).

School sexual harassment has a negative impact on students' emotional and educational lives.

- Nearly half (47 percent) of all students who experience sexual harassment feel very or somewhat upset right afterward.

- Students who experience physical harassment are more likely than those who experience nonphysical harassment to feel very or somewhat upset (56 percent vs. 26 percent).

- Students who experience sexual harassment are most likely to react by avoiding the person who bothered or harassed them (40 percent), talking less in class (24 percent), not wanting to go to school (22 percent), changing their seat in class to get farther away from someone (21 percent), and finding it hard to pay attention in school (20 percent).

Students today are much more likely than those in 1993 to say their schools have a policy or distribute literature on sexual harassment.

- Seven in 10 students (69 percent), compared to just 26 percent in 1993, say their schools have a policy on sexual harassment to deal with sexual harassment issues and complaints.

- More than one-third (36 percent) of students, compared to 13 percent in 1993, say their schools distribute booklets, handouts, and other literature and materials about sexual harassment.

Nearly all students surveyed know what sexual harassment is.

■ Ninety-six percent of students say they know what sexual harassment is.

■ This percentage is higher for students who say their schools both have a policy and distribute materials on sexual harassment than for those who say their schools do neither (98 percent vs. 91 percent).

The most upsetting examples of sexual harassment in school life involve speech as well as actions. Students are most likely to be very upset if someone did the following:

■ Spread sexual rumors about them (75 percent)

■ Pulled off or down their clothing (74 percent)

■ Said they were gay or lesbian (73 percent)

■ Forced them to do something sexual other than kissing (72 percent)

■ Spied on them as they dressed or showered (69 percent)

■ Wrote sexual messages or graffiti about them on bathroom walls, in locker rooms, etc. (63 percent)

A sizeable minority of students reports high levels of sexual harassment in school.

■ Fourteen percent of students say there is a lot of sexual harassment in school.

■ This level has not substantially changed since 1993 (14 percent today; 15 percent in 1993).

Most experiences involve students harassing other students, although many experiences involve school adults harassing students.

■ As in 1993, nearly nine in 10 students (85 percent) report that students sexually harass other students at their schools.

■ A large number of students report that teachers and other school employees sexually harass students, although this number has declined since 1993 (38 percent today vs. 44 percent in 1993).

Slightly more than half (54 percent) of students say they have sexually harassed someone during their school lives.

■ This represents a decline from 1993, when six in 10 students (59 percent) said they sexually harassed someone.

■ In particular, boys today are less likely to report being a perpetrator (57 percent today vs. 66 percent in 1993).

Chapter 1:
Still Hostile Hallways

Nearly all students say they know what sexual harassment is, as they did in 1993. And boys' and girls' definitions of harassment do not differ substantially. These two findings stay the same although students today are more likely than students in 1993 to say their schools have a policy or distribute materials on sexual harassment.

The most common forms of harassment in school, say students, include making sexual comments, jokes, gestures, or looks; spreading sexual rumors; and calling others gay or lesbian. Girls and boys also rank nonphysical forms among the most upsetting types of harassment.

Girls are more likely than boys to assess that there is at least some harassment in school (42 percent vs. 32 percent). One in seven students (14 percent) says there is a lot of harassment. Only nine in 100 (9 percent) report that there is none.

Boys and girls today report, as they did in 1993, that mostly students sexually harass other students. Survey results also show a modest decrease in the number of students who say teachers and other school employees harass students.

Being Afraid at School

A significant minority of students—both boys and girls—fear being hurt by someone in their school lives. These levels of fear have not changed from 1993. Gender, grade level, and race/ethnicity all play roles in students' experiences of fear.

Two in 10 students (18 percent) are afraid some or most of the time that someone will hurt or bother them at school. Boys and girls are equally likely to feel this way, and these levels also do not differ between urban and suburban/rural schools. Eighth- and ninth-grade girls are as likely as 10th- and 11th-grade girls to report being afraid some or most of the time that someone will hurt or bother them. Boys in the lower grades, however, are more likely

than boys in the upper grades to report being afraid (21 percent vs. 13 percent).

Never Being Afraid at School

Less than half (46 percent) of students report never being afraid that someone will hurt or bother them at school. Boys and girls differ in this regard, with boys more likely than girls to report never being afraid (51 percent vs. 40 percent). Race and grade level also differentiate this experience. Black boys (61 percent) and girls (53 percent) are more likely to never be afraid at school than white boys (51 percent) and girls (37 percent).

Awareness of Harassment

Nearly all girls and boys say they know what sexual harassment is (96 percent today; 97 percent in 1993). (See Figure 1.) Gender and race/ethnicity do not distinguish students' level of knowledge. Students who say their schools both have a policy and distribute materials on sexual harassment are more likely than those whose schools do neither to say they know what sexual harassment is (98 percent when schools do both vs. 91 percent when schools do neither).

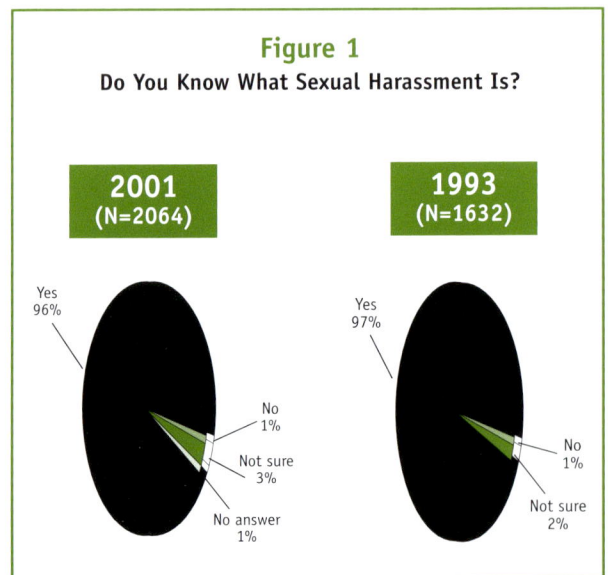

Figure 1
Do You Know What Sexual Harassment Is?

2001
(N=2064)

Yes 96%
No 1%
Not sure 3%
No answer 1%

1993
(N=1632)

Yes 97%
No 1%
Not sure 2%

Base: All respondents

Definitions of Sexual Harassment

When asked open-ended questions, students are most likely to describe harassment as comments or gestures, unspecified (30 percent); unwanted touching, grabbing, or contact (23 percent); touching, grabbing, or contact, unspecified (20 percent); and making someone very uncomfortable (17 percent).

Boys' and girls' definitions of sexual harassment do not differ substantially. In answers to open-ended questions, both boys and girls reference comments, verbal abuse, rumors, and gestures as much as they emphasize unwanted physical actions.

"It's when someone violates you sexually," says an 11th-grade boy. "You can be harassed mentally, physically, or spiritually. Also, the harassment can be through physical contact, audible contact, or written contact." A 10th-grade girl defines sexual harassment similarly: "unwanted touching, name-calling, suggestive looks, gestures, or anything else of a sexual nature." For most students, physical and verbal acts might both constitute harassment if the behavior is unwanted and persistent. "It is any unwanted actions, touching, sounds, jokes, etc., of a sexual nature that make the victim feel uncomfortable," says an 11th-grade girl. Some students place particular emphasis on the intent to make someone feel uncomfortable. Says a 10th-grade girl, "Sexual harassment can be any comment or action that may disturb or embarrass someone, especially if the comment or action is meant to do so."

Similarly, both boys and girls emphasize in their definitions the effects of the action on the victim, whether intended or not, rather than the action itself. For many, sexual harassment connotes verbal

> "[Schools can] have teachers watch more closely to monitor for sexual harassment, because sometimes they see it but don't care."
>
> —10th-grade boy

or physical actions that create discomfort for the subject. These definitions mirror prevalent legal definitions of sexual harassment in the workplace, which emphasize the creation of a hostile work environment through verbal or physical actions that cause discomfort.

A 10th-grade boy defines sexual harassment, for example, as the act of "making someone uncomfortable about their sexuality, or making them uncomfortable about themselves, whether by physical or verbal means." Similarly, a 10th-grade girl emphasizes the effects on the target: "when a person, male or female, is being taunted by another person, male or female, in a way that makes them feel uncomfortable." An 11th-grade boy defines harassment as "anything another person does that makes you feel uncomfortable or uneasy. Can be verbal, emotional, or physical."

When defining sexual harassment, many students emphasize that the behaviors must be unwelcome, unwanted, or unreciprocated. Several male respondents, in particular, define sexual harassment as the persistence of unwanted behaviors even after the subjects make their intentions clear or behaviors and actions that do not mesh with the subjects' desires or wishes.

One ninth-grade boy defines harassment, for example, as "someone forcing themselves on another in a sexual way ... that has no interest in what the other person wants," and a ninth-grade girl says harassment is "when someone puts sexual pressure or comment[s] on you when you're unwilling."

A 10th-grade girl defines harassment as "when someone touches you in a way where you feel uncomfortable or when you know that they are doing something wrong. If you want them to do it, then I don't consider it harassment."

Words and Actions Hurt

Many boys and girls define sexual harassment as comments and gestures, and these nonphysical experiences also appear to be among the most upsetting. (See Figure 2 on page 11.) When given the 14 examples of nonphysical and physical harassment, students are most likely to report that they would be very upset if someone did the following:

- Spread sexual rumors about them (75 percent)
- Pulled off or down their clothing (74 percent)
- Said they were gay or lesbian (73 percent)
- Forced them to do something sexual other than kissing (72 percent)

HOW DO YOU DEFINE SEXUAL HARASSMENT?

❖ "When you say something to someone like, 'hey nice breasts' or call them a 'lesbian.' Whenever you say something about sex to them without their permission, or if they have a problem with it. Trust me. I know what it is." (ninth-grade boy)

❖ "When someone invades your personal body space or privacy." (eighth-grade girl)

❖ "Someone making advances towards me and saying things that make me feel very uncomfortable." (eighth-grade boy)

❖ "It's when someone asks you sexual questions or talks about sex or wants you to have sex with them." (eighth-grade girl)

❖ "Being touched or talked to in any sexual sense that makes you uncomfortable or hurt." (ninth-grade girl)

❖ "Unwanted sexual advances, comments, or demands for sexual favors." (10th-grade boy)

❖ "When someone takes it farther than you want to go. Even hugs and pats on the back can be sexual harassment if the person doesn't want it." (10th-grade boy)

❖ "Sexual harassment can be verbal or nonverbal. If somebody is commenting on your features or using obscenities, it is verbal. It is nonverbal if they are actually touching you when you do not want to be." (10th-grade boy)

❖ "When a guy continues to make you feel awkward in a sexual way." (10th-grade girl)

❖ "Sexual harassment is when a person 'either sex' makes comments on sexuality or about having sex in a way that offends or makes you uncomfortable." (10th-grade girl)

❖ "Harassment that is always taking place on the male to female but never the other way." (11th-grade boy)

❖ "When someone touches, says, looks at you either when you stop or didn't want it in the first place. Stuff that is just not appropriate: touching, kissing, taking pictures of, yelling." (11th-grade girl)

❖ "Feminist-politically correct language for saying things like 'hello good-looking.'" (11th-grade boy)

❖ "Using threats for sex. (I'll fire you unless you ...) Bothering someone with either unwelcomed sexual actions or language." (11th-grade boy)

❖ "Any unwanted attention." (11th-grade girl)

❖ "Touching that you don't want." (11th-grade girl)

Figure 2
How Upset Would You Be If Someone Did This to You? (% Saying Very)

Action	Boys	Girls
Made sexual comments, jokes, gestures, or looks	11%	24%
Showed, gave, or left you sexual pictures, photographs, illustrations, messages, or notes	19%	53%
Wrote sexual messages/graffiti about you on bathroom walls, in locker rooms, etc.	53%	74%
Spread sexual rumors about you	63%	88%
Said you were gay or lesbian	74%	73%
Spied on you as you dressed or showered at school	55%	85%
Flashed or "mooned" you	22%	28%
Touched, grabbed, or pinched you in a sexual way	35%	62%
Intentionally brushed up against you in a sexual way	24%	44%
Pulled at your clothing in a sexual way	28%	59%
Pulled off or down your clothing	59%	91%
Blocked your way or cornered you in a sexual way	38%	64%
Forced you to kiss him/her	46%	79%
Forced you to do something sexual other than kissing	54%	92%

■ Boys (N=970) ■ Girls (N=1094)

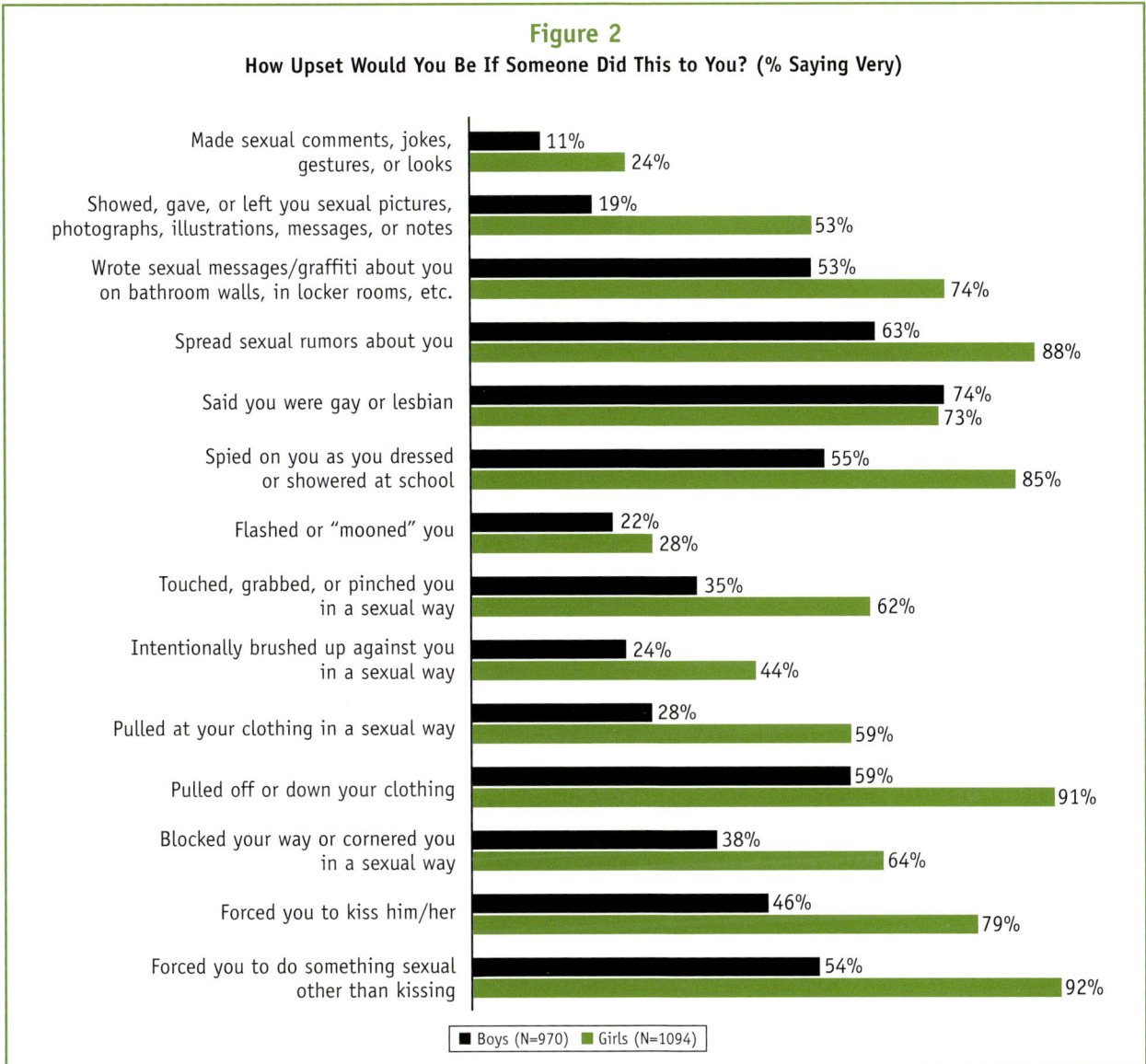

Base: All respondents

■ Spied on them as they dressed or showered at school (69 percent)

■ Wrote sexual messages or graffiti about them on bathroom walls, in locker rooms, etc. (63 percent)

Four of these six most upsetting acts involve no physical contact, affirming the hurtful potential of words and rumors. Girls are consistently more likely than boys to say they would be very upset by all 14 of the incidents, with one notable exception: Boys (74 percent) and girls (73 percent) are almost equally likely to say they would be very upset if someone called them gay or lesbian.

Changes Since 1993

Students today are less likely than those in 1993 to say they would be very upset by many of these

Figure 3
What Is the Level of Harassment at School?

	Total	Gender		Size of Place		School's Commitment		
		Boys	Girls	Urban	Suburban/ Rural	Policy & Handouts	Policy or Handouts	Neither
Base:	2064	970	1094	733	1331	714	863	456
	%	%	%	%	%	%	%	%
A lot	14	13	16	17	13	15	14	14
Some but not a lot	37	32	42	35	37	38	39	31
Only a little	24	28	20	23	25	26	23	24
Not any	9	9	8	10	8	7	9	10
Not sure	12	14	10	12	12	9	11	17
No answer	4	4	3	3	4	4	3	4

Base: All respondents

Figure 4
What Is the Level of Harassment at School (by Race/Ethnicity and Gender)?

	Total	Race/Ethnicity (Boys)			Race/Ethnicity (Girls)		
		White	Black	Hispanic	White	Black	Hispanic
Base:	2064	547	179	170	604	211	213
	%	%	%	%	%	%	%
A lot	14	14	15	12	16	19	13
Some but not a lot	37	33	35	24	44	42	36
Only a little	24	27	26	29	22	12	17
Not any	9	10	5	9	5	9	17
Not sure	12	13	13	19	8	16	13
No answer	4	3	5	8	4	3	3

Base: All respondents

experiences. The largest differences relate to feelings about being called gay or lesbian—73 percent would feel upset today vs. 86 percent in 1993—and being touched, grabbed, or pinched in a sexual way—48 percent vs. 56 percent.

Although the degree to which students find these experiences upsetting has changed since 1993, students' ranking of the most and least upsetting experiences has not. As in 1993, students today are most likely to say they would be very upset by someone spreading sexual rumors about them, pulling off or down their clothing, or calling them gay or lesbian. They are least likely to say they would be very upset by someone intentionally brushing up against them in a sexual way, flashing

or "mooning" them, or making sexual comments, jokes, gestures, or looks.

Frequency of Harassment

After setting out the definition and examples of sexual harassment (see Executive Summary and Major Findings), the survey asked students to assess the levels of harassment in their school.

Although students today are more likely than students in 1993 to say their schools have a policy or distribute materials on sexual harassment, there has been little change in students' report of the frequency of harassment. One in seven students (14 percent) reports a lot of sexual harassment in school or related to school life. Nine in 100 (9 percent) say there is none. (See Figure 3 on page 12.) These levels do not differ substantially by gender, race/ethnicity, urban or suburban/rural, or grade level.

Girls, however, are more likely than boys to say there is some but not a lot of sexual harassment (42 percent vs. 32 percent). Race/ethnicity also seems to influence this response. Hispanic boys and girls are less likely than their white and black peers to report that there is some but not a lot of harassment in their schools (24 percent for Hispanic vs. 33 percent for white and 35 percent for black boys; 36 percent for Hispanic vs. 44 percent for white and 42 percent for black girls). (See Figure 4 on page 12.) Also of interest is the finding that students who say their schools both have a sexual harassment policy and distribute

materials are more likely than those who say their schools do neither to report that there is some harassment in their schools (38 percent vs. 31 percent).

Has It Happened to Someone You Know

Students are most likely to report that someone at school has done the following to someone they know personally:

■ Made sexual comments, jokes, gestures, or looks (71 percent)

■ Said they were gay or lesbian (61 percent)

■ Spread sexual rumors about them (61 percent)

■ Touched, grabbed, or pinched them in a sexual way (60 percent)

Figure 5
Has Someone Done This to Someone You Know? (% Saying Yes)

	Total	Gender		Size of Place		School's Commitment		
		Boys	Girls	Urban	Suburban/ Rural	Policy & Handouts	Policy or Handouts	Neither
Base:	1559	751	808	563	996	496	633	399
	%	%	%	%	%	%	%	%
Made sexual comments, jokes, gestures, or looks	71	67	77	72	71	72	73	68
Showed, gave, or left them sexual pictures, photographs, illustrations, messages, or notes	36	39	32	34	36	38	35	34
Wrote sexual messages/graffiti about them on bathroom walls, in locker rooms, etc.	37	31	44	34	39	39	35	37
Spread sexual rumors about them	61	51	72	61	61	63	63	56
Said they were gay or lesbian	61	58	64	63	60	59	66	56
Spied on them as they dressed or showered at school	13	13	13	16	11	12	14	11
Flashed or "mooned" them	55	53	57	52	56	59	55	48
Touched, grabbed, or pinched them in a sexual way	60	52	68	63	58	62	61	54
Intentionally brushed up against them in a sexual way	53	49	56	56	51	55	54	47
Pulled at their clothing in a sexual way	35	34	35	36	34	36	38	28
Pulled off or down their clothing	23	24	23	22	24	24	26	17
Blocked their way or cornered them in a sexual way	29	23	36	30	29	32	30	24
Forced them to kiss her/him	23	20	25	25	22	22	24	22
Forced them to do something sexual other than kissing	15	14	17	17	15	16	15	14

Base: In-school respondents

Figure 6
Who Harasses Whom?

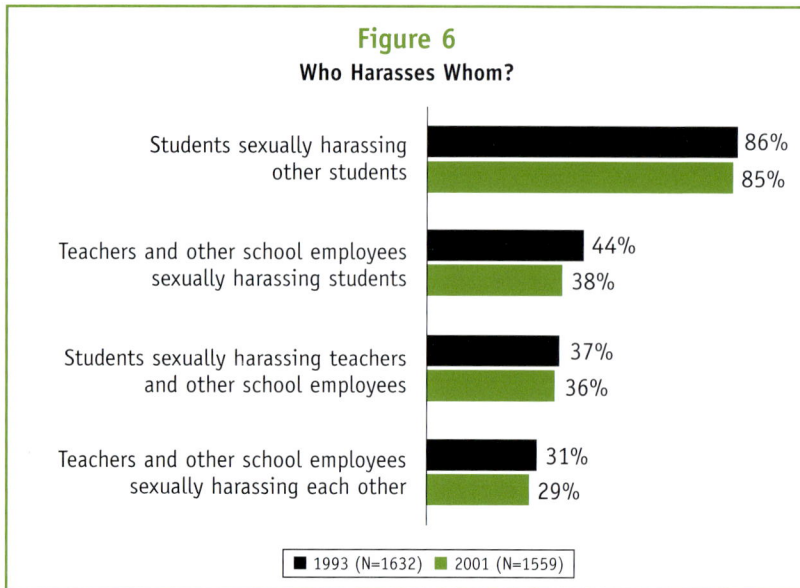

	1993 (N=1632)	2001 (N=1559)
Students sexually harassing other students	86%	85%
Teachers and other school employees sexually harassing students	44%	38%
Students sexually harassing teachers and other school employees	37%	36%
Teachers and other school employees sexually harassing each other	31%	29%

Base: In-school respondents

- Flashed or "mooned" them (55 percent)
- Intentionally brushed up against them in a sexual way (53 percent)

Overall, girls are more likely than boys to know someone personally who has had these experiences at school. (See Figure 5 on page 13.)

The second most common experience—students saying that someone they know has been called gay or lesbian—saw the biggest increase, from 51 percent in 1993 to 61 percent today. Most other experiences have remained steady or decreased. Students are less likely today than in 1993, for instance, to say they know someone who has had their clothing pulled off or down (23 percent vs. 32 percent) or had sexual messages or graffiti written about them (37 percent vs. 45 percent).

Who Harasses: Students and Teachers

Fewer respondents today than in 1993 say teachers and other school employees sexually harass students (38 percent today vs. 44 percent in 1993). (See Figure 6.) More often, respondents say students

harass other students (85 percent today; 86 percent in 1993).

Girls are slightly more likely than boys to report harassment, both by other students (88 percent vs. 83 percent) and by teachers and other employees (41 percent vs. 36 percent).

Race/ethnicity differentiates students' reporting of teachers and other school employees sexually harassing students: White students are more likely than Hispanic students to report this occurrence (44 percent of white girls and 37 percent of white boys vs. 32 percent of Hispanic girls and 26 percent of Hispanic boys). And students who say their schools have a sexual harassment policy and distribute materials are more likely than those who say their schools do neither to report student-on-student harassment (88 percent vs. 78 percent).

Girls' and boys' assessments of the school climate generally mirror their accounts of personal experiences with harassment (see Chapter 2). Yet interestingly, the survey also shows that students perceive that teachers and other school adults harass students more than they report personally experiencing this type of harassment.

Who Would Students Tell

Not even half (40 percent) of students say they would be likely to complain to a school adult if they were sexually harassed by another student. This represents a slight increase over 1993, a difference wholly accounted for by a change in girls' responses: up from 43 percent in 1993 to 52 percent today. Overall, girls are more likely than boys to say they would complain to a school employee (52 percent vs. 29 percent). (See Figure 7 on page 15.) Broken down by gender and race/ethnicity, black girls are more likely than white girls to say they would complain to a school employee about another student (59 percent vs. 49 percent).

By comparison, 71 percent of students say they would complain to a school adult if they were sexually harassed by a teacher or other school employee. This level has remained about the same since 1993. That number is higher for girls than for boys (76 percent vs. 67 percent). (See Figure 8.) Students who report that their schools both have a policy and distribute handouts are more likely than students who report that their schools do neither to say they would complain (75 percent vs. 67 percent). Broken down by gender and race/ethnicity, white boys are more likely than black boys to say they would complain to a school employee about harassment by a teacher or other employee (71 percent vs. 49 percent).

This picture looks somewhat different when girls and boys describe their personal experiences with harassment (see Chapter 2). In reality, fewer students say they actually told a teacher or other employee when they were harassed.

Awareness of School Policies and Materials

The greatest change during the past eight years appears to be students' increased awareness of their schools' policies and materials to address sexual harassment. Seven in 10 students today (69 percent) report that their schools have a policy on sexual harassment to deal with issues and complaints. More than one-third (36 percent) say their schools distribute booklets, handouts, and other literature and materials about sexual harassment. These figures represent a sea change since 1993, when only one-quarter (26 percent) of students said their schools have a sexual harassment policy and 13 percent said their schools give out literature and materials about sexual harassment.

In 1993 nearly six in 10 students (57 percent) were not sure whether their schools had a sexual harassment policy, compared to two in 10 (22 percent) today. A similar trend exists in students' awareness of their schools' distribution of materials: 37 percent were unsure in 1993 compared to 28 percent today. (See Figure 9 on page 16.)

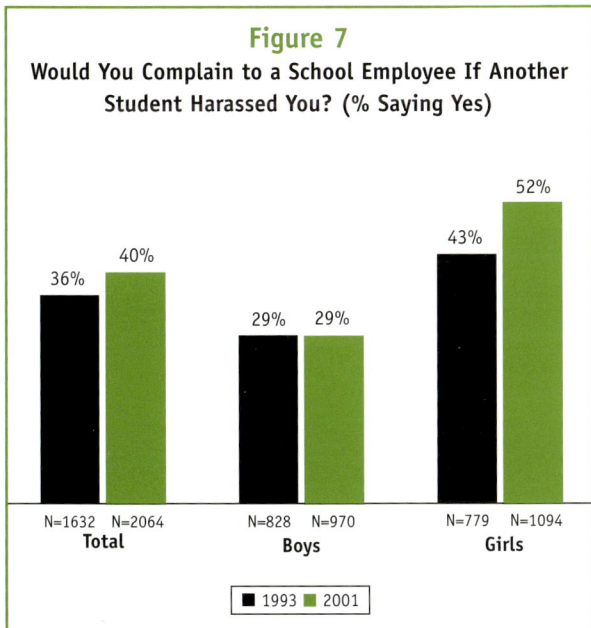

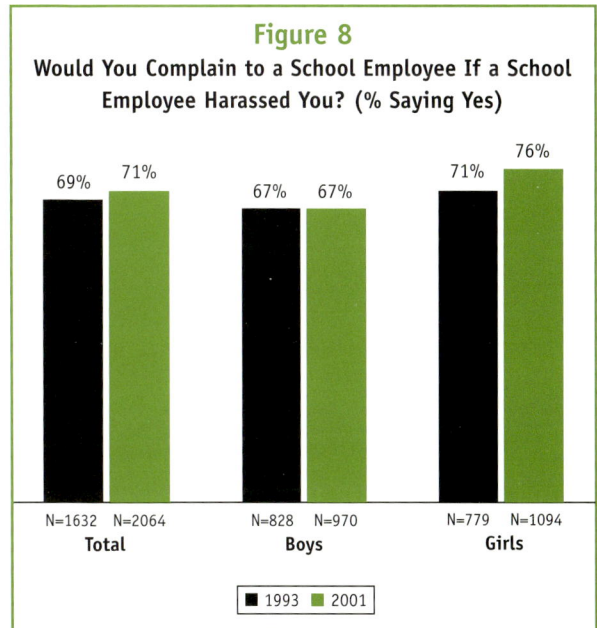

Figure 7
Would You Complain to a School Employee If Another Student Harassed You? (% Saying Yes)

	Total		Boys		Girls	
1993	36%		29%		43%	
2001		40%		29%		52%
N	N=1632	N=2064	N=828	N=970	N=779	N=1094

■ 1993 ■ 2001

Base: All respondents

Figure 8
Would You Complain to a School Employee If a School Employee Harassed You? (% Saying Yes)

	Total		Boys		Girls	
1993	69%		67%		71%	
2001		71%		67%		76%
N	N=1632	N=2064	N=828	N=970	N=779	N=1094

■ 1993 ■ 2001

Base: All respondents

Figure 9

Does Your School Have a Sexual Harassment Policy?

2001 (N=2064)

- No 8%
- Yes 69%
- Not sure 22%
- No answer 1%

1993 (N=1632)

- No 17%
- Yes 26%
- Not sure 57%

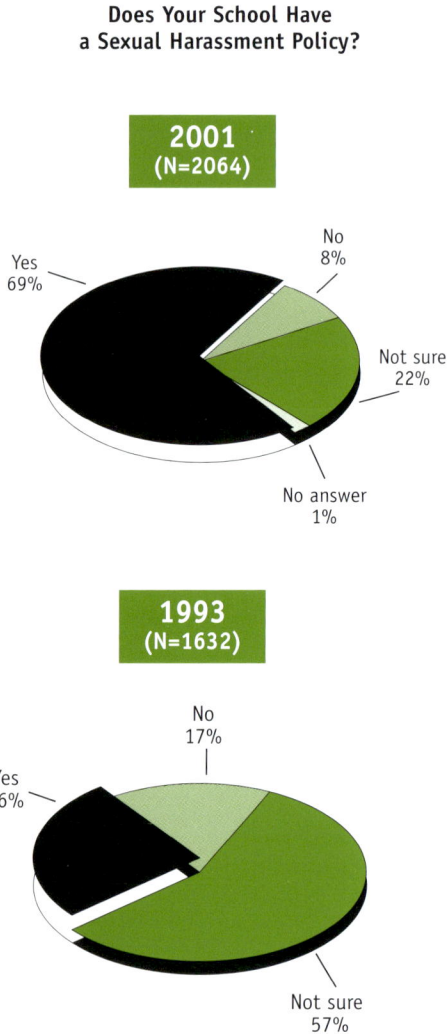

Base: All respondents

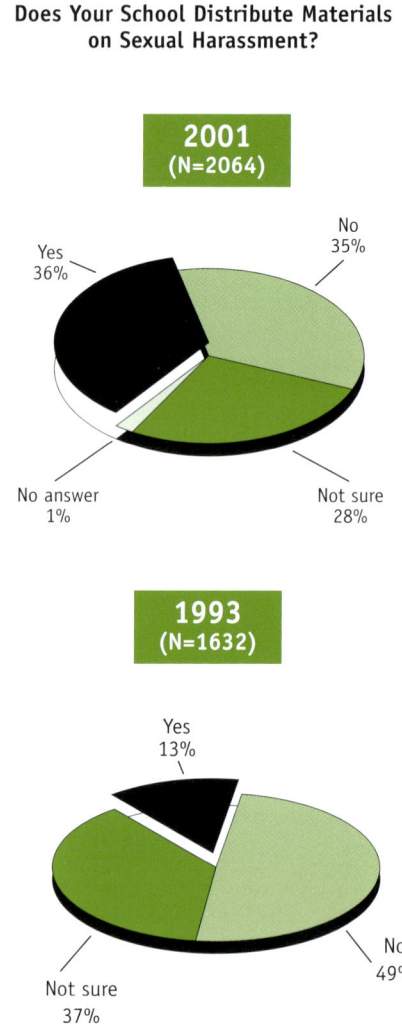

Does Your School Distribute Materials on Sexual Harassment?

2001 (N=2064)

- No 35%
- Yes 36%
- Not sure 28%
- No answer 1%

1993 (N=1632)

- Yes 13%
- No 49%
- Not sure 37%

Base: All respondents

Of particular interest, boys are more likely than girls to be aware that their schools have a policy on sexual harassment (72 percent vs. 66 percent) and slightly more likely to say their schools distribute materials on sexual harassment (38 percent vs. 34 percent). Students' awareness of their schools' policies and activities does not differ by race/ethnicity, and students in upper grades are only slightly more likely than those in lower grades to report that their schools distribute materials on sexual harassment (39 percent vs. 34 percent).

Students' Suggestions and Recommendations

Students offer schools a variety of suggestions to raise awareness about and deal with sexual harassment. Fifteen percent suggest classes, seminars, assemblies, or speakers. Nine percent recommend better enforcement and understanding of existing policies and stricter or swifter consequences. Some in this latter category note preferential treatment for athletes or other students, and others complain that adults do not observe students' actions, genuinely listen to students, or take the issue seriously.

Some respondents say that their schools already hold assemblies or show videos and that these activities do not appreciably change the school climate or students' behavior. "Anything but show videos," says one eighth-grade girl. Recommends another eighth-grade girl: "Instead of popping in a video and expecting the problem to be solved, teachers need to take time out and TALK to us. It's a problem that one video can't fix." A third eighth-grade girl suggests, "Have teachers teach more about it and not just blow off complaints." Says a ninth-grade girl, "I would like to see them observe what is going on."

Others write that students may not understand or recognize the characteristics of sexual harassment or its effects. "I think they should help distinguish a little more the differences between sexual harassment and accidents," comments one 10th-grade boy. A ninth-grade girl recommends assemblies "to raise awareness of what it does to people instead of telling us about drugs all the time!"

One in 11 students (9 percent) reports that their schools already deal effectively with this issue. "I think my school has done plenty. The people who attend my school are the problem," an 11th-grade boy remarks. Says a ninth-grade girl, "The schools do the best they can." One in seven (14 percent) say nothing should be done. Some students in this category express concern that policies may become draconian and unduly punitive. "We get in trouble for calling someone 'sexy,' so I think the school needs to ease up on some stuff," an 11th-grade boy writes.

WHAT COULD YOUR SCHOOL DO TO ADDRESS SEXUAL HARASSMENT?

❖ "Maybe if they had an assembly about sexual harassment and expulsion for those who violate rules." (eighth-grade boy)

❖ "My school handles the issue of sexual harassment very well." (eighth-grade girl)

❖ "I'd just like them to, if the matter comes up, deal with it swiftly and fairly, taking in all considerations." (ninth-grade girl)

❖ "Stop letting athletes get off easy." (ninth-grade boy)

❖ "Deal with the problem on the spot." (10th-grade girl)

❖ "Make aware what exactly it is and what to do about it if you are offended." (10th-grade boy)

❖ "Come on … it's big deal out of nothing." (10th-grade boy)

❖ "Nothing more, they do plenty." (10th-grade boy)

❖ "Have the same no tolerance policy as knives or guns and make an example of anyone who does commit sexual harassment, so maybe it will stop others." (11th-grade girl)

❖ "Maybe have an awareness week." (11th-grade girl)

❖ "Seminars, a definite policy in the handbook." (11th-grade girl)

❖ "I think that the current policies that deal with that subject are sufficient enough for the quantity and the degree of offense found at my high school." (11th-grade boy)

❖ "Nothing. It's getting a little bit out of hand." (11th-grade boy)

Chapter 2:
Personal Experiences
With Sexual Harassment

As in 1993, eight in 10 students (81 percent) report having experienced some form of harassment in their school lives. Since 1993, however, the "gender gap" in harassment has slightly narrowed. Sexual harassment was a more common occurrence for girls than boys in 1993, but today this difference has decreased.

Both nonphysical and physical harassment are prevalent. The most common experience is being the target of sexual comments, jokes, gestures, or looks, an occurrence experienced by two-thirds of all students. The second most common experience is being touched, grabbed, or pinched in a sexual way. Nearly half (49 percent) of all students report this type of harassment: 57 percent of girls and 42 percent of boys.

Students' personal experiences with harassment reveal that the problem begins at a young age. More than one-third (35 percent) of students who experience harassment report their first occurrence in sixth grade or earlier.

One-third (32 percent) of students fear being sexually harassed during school, with Hispanic boys and girls more likely to report being afraid than their peers in other racial/ethnic groups.

The vast majority of all harassment, physical and nonphysical, occurs between students, and most occurs in halls, classrooms, the gym area, or outside on school grounds.

Although both boys and girls report awareness of sexual harassment policies and procedures, students are six times more likely to tell a friend than a teacher or other school employee about their experience with harassment.

How Often It Happens

As in 1993, eight in 10 students (81 percent) say they personally experience sexual harassment in their school lives often, occasionally, or rarely. (See Figure 10.) In 1993 girls were much more likely than boys to have ever experienced sexual harassment. The gender gap was 85 percent vs. 76 percent

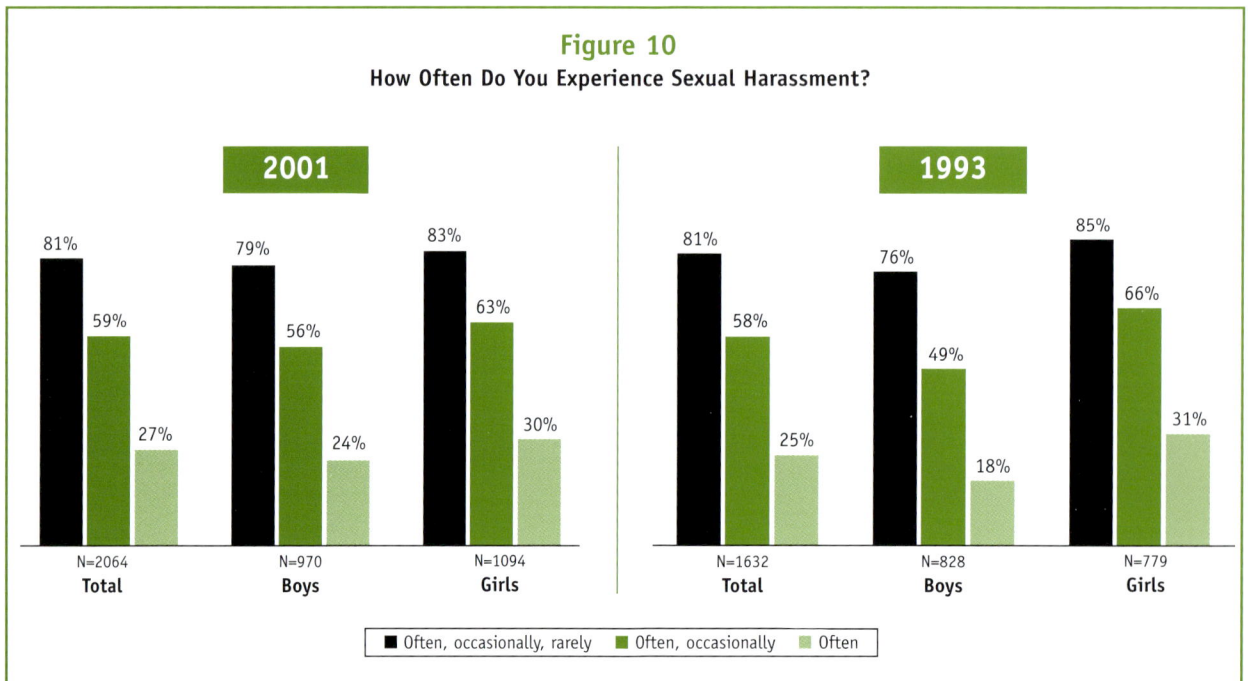

Figure 10
How Often Do You Experience Sexual Harassment?

Base: All respondents

eight years ago (girls vs. boys); today it has narrowed to 83 percent vs. 79 percent.

A majority of students often or occasionally experience school sexual harassment (59 percent today; 58 percent in 1993). And, as in 1993, one in four students reports that they often experience some form of sexual harassment (27 percent today; 25 percent in 1993). A smaller minority—14 percent —says they experience a lot of harassment in their school lives.

> "One classmate liked to say that I have BIG BREASTS and went around trying to squeeze them."
>
> —ninth-grade girl

Types of Harassment Students Experience

The most common forms of school sexual harassment span the nonphysical and physical:

- Making sexual comments, jokes, gestures, or looks (66 percent today; 66 percent in 1993)

- Touching, grabbing, or pinching in a sexual way (49 percent today; 53 percent in 1993)

- Intentionally brushing up against them in a sexual way (47 percent today; 46 percent in 1993)

- Flashing or "mooning" (43 percent today; 45 percent in 1993)

Boys today more often experience sexual harassment than boys surveyed in 1993. The biggest change in the type of harassment experienced from 1993 to today is the incidence of students being called gay or lesbian: a jump from 17 percent in 1993 to 36 percent today. Boys today are more than twice as likely to say they have often or occasionally been called gay or lesbian (9 percent in 1993 vs. 19 percent today). Girls are nearly three times more likely to be called gay or lesbian (5 percent in 1993 vs. 13 percent today).

Boys are also more likely today to say someone has intentionally brushed up against them in a sexual

way (20 percent vs. 15 percent). Girls are less likely to be touched, grabbed, or pinched in a sexual way (29 percent vs. 40 percent) or to be the targets of sexual comments, jokes, gestures, or looks (48 percent vs. 53 percent). (See Figure 11 on page 22 and Figure 12 on page 23.)

Personal Experiences of Nonphysical Harassment

Although students' experiences with nonphysical harassment today do not differ by whether the school they attend is urban or suburban/ rural, gender and race/ethnicity do play a role. Girls are more likely than boys to be the target of sexual comments, jokes, gestures, or looks (73 percent vs. 59 percent) and sexual rumors (39 percent vs. 32 percent) or to be flashed or "mooned" (45 percent vs. 40 percent). Boys more than girls say someone called them gay or lesbian (42 percent vs. 29 percent) or showed, gave, or left them sexual photographs, illustrations, messages, or notes (35 percent vs. 28 percent).

White boys are more likely than black boys to report that at some time in their school lives someone called them gay or lesbian (45 percent vs. 30 percent) or flashed or "mooned" them (44 percent vs. 26 percent). Hispanic boys are more likely than black boys to say they were the target of sexual jokes, comments, gestures, or looks (56 percent vs. 39 percent).

White girls are more likely than Hispanic girls to say someone spread sexual rumors about them (42 percent vs. 29 percent) or flashed or "mooned" them (47 percent vs. 36 percent). And white girls are more likely than black girls to say someone called them gay or lesbian (32 percent vs. 20 percent). Grade level, however, does not distinguish students' experiences with nonphysical sexual harassment.

Figure 11
Has Anyone Done This to You Often or Occasionally—Boys?

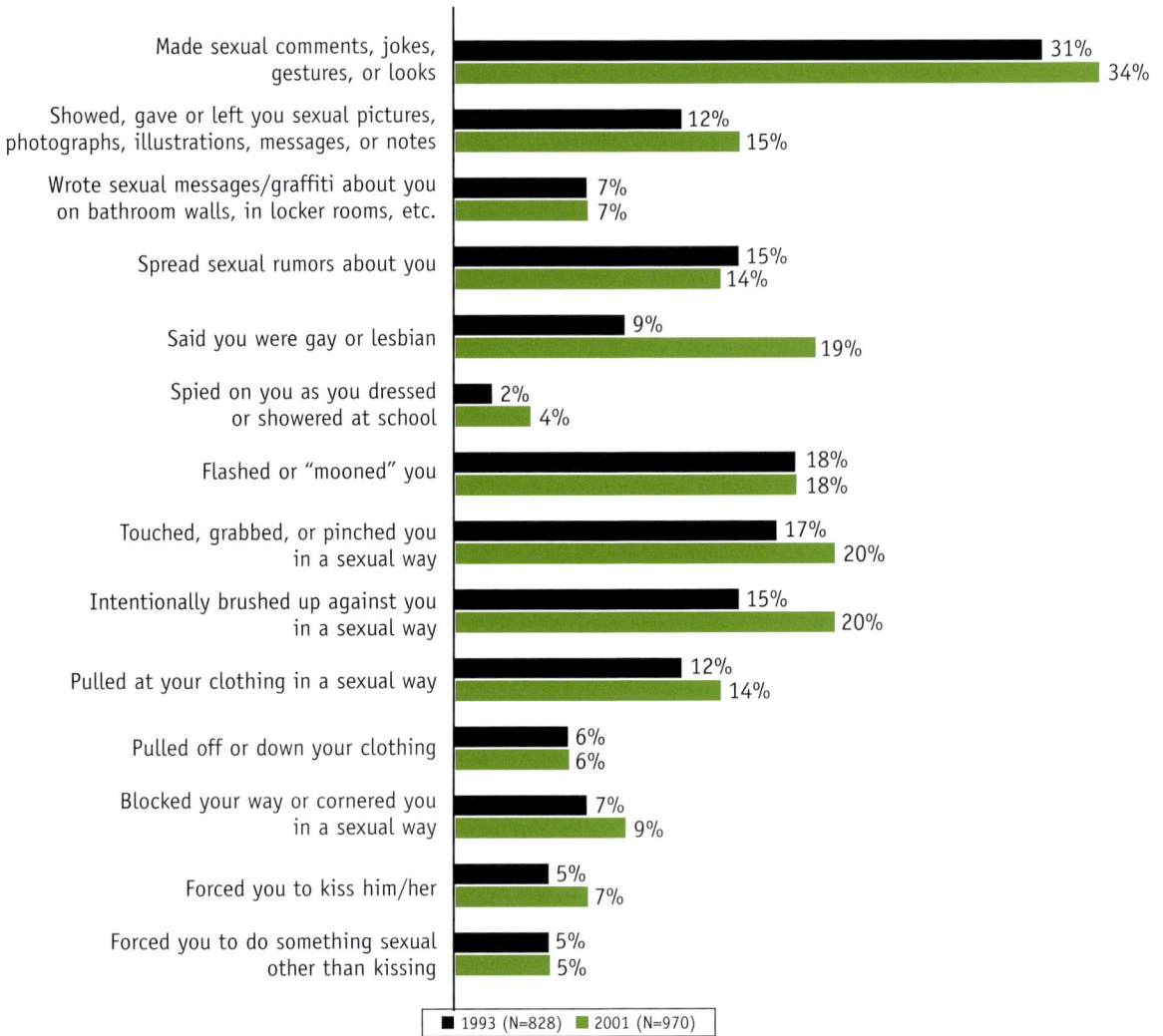

Category	1993 (N=828)	2001 (N=970)
Made sexual comments, jokes, gestures, or looks	31%	34%
Showed, gave or left you sexual pictures, photographs, illustrations, messages, or notes	12%	15%
Wrote sexual messages/graffiti about you on bathroom walls, in locker rooms, etc.	7%	7%
Spread sexual rumors about you	15%	14%
Said you were gay or lesbian	9%	19%
Spied on you as you dressed or showered at school	2%	4%
Flashed or "mooned" you	18%	18%
Touched, grabbed, or pinched you in a sexual way	17%	20%
Intentionally brushed up against you in a sexual way	15%	20%
Pulled at your clothing in a sexual way	12%	14%
Pulled off or down your clothing	6%	6%
Blocked your way or cornered you in a sexual way	7%	9%
Forced you to kiss him/her	5%	7%
Forced you to do something sexual other than kissing	5%	5%

■ 1993 (N=828) ■ 2001 (N=970)

Base: All boys

Overall, students' experiences of nonphysical sexual harassment have not changed since 1993, whether calculated by those reporting often, occasional, or rare experiences (76 percent today; 77 percent in 1993) or often or occasional experiences (54 percent today; 52 percent in 1993). Boys today, however, are more likely to often or occasionally experience some form of nonphysical sexual harassment (50 percent today vs. 43 percent in 1993).

Personal Experiences of Physical Harassment

The most common experiences of physical sexual harassment are being touched, grabbed, or pinched in a sexual way (49 percent) and being intentionally brushed up against in a sexual way (47 percent). Girls are more likely than boys to experience four of the seven examples of physical sexual harassment:

Figure 12
Has Anyone Done This to You Often or Occasionally—Girls?

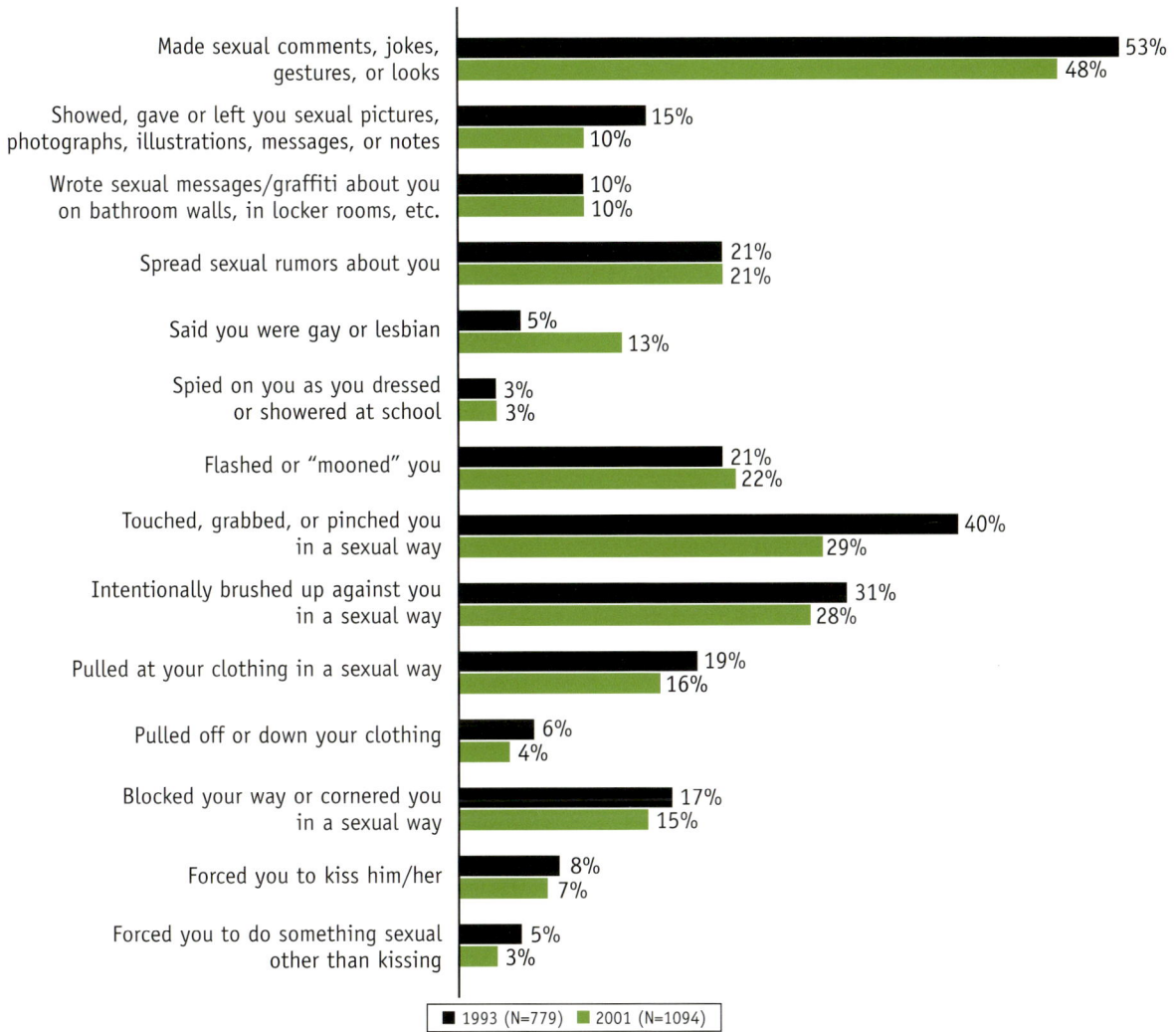

Behavior	1993	2001
Made sexual comments, jokes, gestures, or looks	53%	48%
Showed, gave or left you sexual pictures, photographs, illustrations, messages, or notes	15%	10%
Wrote sexual messages/graffiti about you on bathroom walls, in locker rooms, etc.	10%	10%
Spread sexual rumors about you	21%	21%
Said you were gay or lesbian	5%	13%
Spied on you as you dressed or showered at school	3%	3%
Flashed or "mooned" you	21%	22%
Touched, grabbed, or pinched you in a sexual way	40%	29%
Intentionally brushed up against you in a sexual way	31%	28%
Pulled at your clothing in a sexual way	19%	16%
Pulled off or down your clothing	6%	4%
Blocked your way or cornered you in a sexual way	17%	15%
Forced you to kiss him/her	8%	7%
Forced you to do something sexual other than kissing	5%	3%

■ 1993 (N=779) ■ 2001 (N=1094)

Base: All girls

- Touched, grabbed, or pinched in a sexual way (57 percent girls vs. 42 percent boys)
- Intentionally brushed up against in a sexual way (53 percent girls vs. 42 percent boys)
- Clothing pulled at in a sexual way (34 percent girls vs. 28 percent boys)
- Blocked or cornered in a sexual way (34 percent girls vs. 23 percent boys)

Boys and girls are equally likely to be forced to kiss someone (7 percent). Boys are more likely than girls, however, to have someone pull off or down their clothing (19 percent vs. 12 percent) or force them to do something sexual other than kissing (12 percent vs. 9 percent).

Size of place also plays a role in certain experiences of physical sexual harassment. Specifically, students in urban schools are more likely than those in sub-urban/rural schools to have someone intentionally brush up against them in a sexual way (51 percent vs. 45 percent).

In terms of racial/ethnic differences, white boys are more likely than their black counterparts to have

someone pull off or down their clothing (21 percent vs. 12 percent).

Black girls are more likely than Hispanic or white girls to be touched, grabbed, or pinched in a sexual way (67 percent for black vs. 51 percent for Hispanic and 56 percent for white), to have someone pull at their

WHAT WAS YOUR MOST RECENT EXPERIENCE WITH SEXUAL HARASSMENT?

Boys

❖ "A girl pulled down my shorts, exposing my boxers, and then kissed me." (eighth-grader)

❖ "Being called fat and gay." (eighth-grader)

❖ "Some idiot jocks called me gay ... they use that as a generic slam for anyone that's different than them." (10th-grader)

❖ "Girls hug me without me wanting to occasionally." (eighth-grader)

❖ "Girls spreading rumors about me." (eighth-grader)

❖ "A girl smacked my butt." (ninth-grader)

❖ "I was asked to go the bathroom to have sex with a girl." (10th-grader)

❖ "I was 'mooned' by my friend." (10th-grader)

❖ "This girl grabbed my penis." (10th-grader)

❖ "A young teacher looking at me." (11th-grader)

❖ "A gay person made comments of having sexual relations with me." (11th-grader)

❖ "An attempt to kiss me ... it was unwanted, and I made that clear." (11th-grader)

Girls

❖ "Someone made a motion like they were masturbating." (eighth-grader)

❖ "Stares when I wear tight clothes." (ninth-grader)

❖ "Being forced to kiss someone." (ninth-grader)

❖ "I guess a 'look' ... he was staring down my shirt and it made me feel uncomfortable." (10th-grader)

❖ "This girl I know started a rumor that I slept with this guy while he was dating my friend." (10th-grader)

❖ "I walked down the hall today, while some moronic guy whistled and said 'Nice breasts, baby.'" (10th-grader)

❖ "A guy slapped my butt when walking down a crowded hall." (11th-grader)

❖ "Someone drew a penis on my notebook." (11th-grader)

❖ "At lunch, a couple of boys at my table started talking about my dog and how they think I have sex with my dog. The longer they talked the nastier they got. I don't sit at that table anymore for lunch." (11th-grader)

Figure 13
Do You Fear Being Sexually Harassed at School?

	Total	Gender		Size of Place	
		Boys	Girls	Urban	Suburban/ Rural
Base:	1559	751	808	563	996
	%	%	%	%	%
Often/Occasionally/Rarely (net)	32	20	44	36	29
Often/Occasionally (net)	11	6	15	12	10
Often	4	3	4	5	3
Occasionally	7	3	11	8	7
Rarely	21	14	29	24	20
Never	63	74	51	58	65
Not sure	3	2	3	2	3
No answer	3	4	2	3	3

Base: In-school respondents

clothing in a sexual way (50 percent for black vs. 30 percent for Hispanic and 32 percent for white) and to be forced to kiss someone (28 percent for black vs. 18 percent for Hispanic and 15 percent for white).

Grade level also matters. Tenth- and 11th-graders are more likely than eighth- and ninth-graders to experience physical harassment (61 percent vs. 55 percent). That increase is greatest for boys: 56 percent for 10th- and 11th-graders vs. 48 percent for eighth- and ninth-graders. By comparison, 66 percent of 10th- and 11th-grade girls and 63 percent of eighth- and ninth-grade girls experience physical harassment.

Overall, students' experiences of physical sexual harassment—whether often, occasional, or rare—show a slight trend of decreasing from 1993, from 61 percent to 58 percent today. Girls' experiences appear to drive this change, down from 72 percent in 1993 to 64 percent today.

First Experiences

Sexual harassment is not just a problem for secondary school students. As in 1993, one-third (35 percent today; 33 percent in 1993) who experience sexual harassment say they first experienced it in elementary school: sixth grade or before. Girls are slightly more likely than boys to say their first experience occurred in elementary school (38 percent vs. 32 percent).

Fear of Being Harassed

One-third (32 percent) of students fear being sexually harassed during school-related times: 20 percent for boys and more than twice that —44 percent—for girls. Students in urban schools are more likely than those in suburban/rural schools to be afraid (36 percent vs. 29 percent). (See Figure 13.)

Race/ethnicity also differentiates experiences. Hispanic boys are more likely than white and black boys to report being afraid often, occasionally, or rarely (25 percent for Hispanic vs. 18 percent for white and 14 percent for black). A similar difference is found among girls (49 percent for Hispanic vs. 43 percent for white and 38 percent for black).

One in nine students (11 percent) is often or occasionally afraid of being sexually harassed during school. Girls are more likely than boys to be often or occasionally afraid (6 percent for boys vs. 15 percent for girls). Fewer girls today than in 1993, however, feel this way (15 percent vs. 22 percent).

Who Harasses Students

The vast majority of all harassment, nonphysical and physical, occurs between students.

Girls who experience any kind of sexual harassment most often report one-on-one, male-to-female harassment. Boys are most likely to be sexually harassed by one other girl or an all-female group.

Among students who report experiencing nonphysical harassment, more than half (52 percent)

Figure 14
Who Harassed You (Nonphysical Harassment) (by Race/Ethnicity and Gender)?

	Total	Race/Ethnicity (Boys)			Race/Ethnicity (Girls)		
		White	Black	Hispanic	White	Black	Hispanic
Base:	1128	259	110	93	304	153	145
	%	%	%	%	%	%	%
One male	52	34	6	14	73	71	70
One female	31	51	52	50	12	14	12
More than one male	36	20	2	14	55	48	50
More than one female	22	38	49	31	6	4	5
More than one person (both males and females)	15	22	4	12	13	7	12

Base: In-school respondents who experienced nonphysical harassment

report being harassed by one male. This scenario is much more common for girls than for boys (73 percent vs. 28 percent). Black boys are less likely than white and Hispanic boys to be harassed by one male (6 percent black vs. 34 percent white and 14 percent Hispanic). About one-third (31 percent) of students are harassed by one female, a scenario much more common for boys than for girls (52 percent vs. 12 percent). (See Figures 14 and 15.)

Three-quarters (76 percent) of students who experience nonphysical sexual harassment are harassed by a student. Girls are more likely than boys to be harassed by a student (85 percent vs. 67 percent) or a former student (44 percent vs. 33 percent). In contrast, 7 percent of students are harassed

Figure 15
Who Harassed You (Nonphysical Harassment)?

	Total	Gender	
		Boys	Girls
Base:	1128	496	632
	%	%	%
One male	52	28	73
One female	31	52	12
More than one male	36	17	53
More than one female	22	39	6
More than one person (both males and females)	15	19	12

Base: In-school respondents who experienced nonphysical harassment

Figure 16
Who Harassed You (Physical Harassment) (by Race/Ethnicity and Gender)?

	Total	Race/Ethnicity (Boys)			Race/Ethnicity (Girls)		
		White	Black	Hispanic	White	Black	Hispanic
Base:	869	181	89	68	238	130	110
	%	%	%	%	%	%	%
One male	57	31	6	15	85	80	82
One female	35	63	63	58	11	13	12
More than one male	36	17	2	8	54	57	57
More than one female	21	44	50	34	4	*	2
More than one person (both males and females)	14	22	5	11	11	7	17

Base: In-school respondents who experienced physical harassment

Figure 17
Who Harassed You
(Physical Harassment)?

	Total	Gender	
		Boys	Girls
Base:	869	366	503
	%	%	%
One male	57	25	84
One female	35	63	12
More than one male	36	14	55
More than one female	21	43	3
More than one person (both males and females)	14	18	11

Base: In-school respondents who experienced physical harassment

by teachers, with boys and girls equally likely to have this experience.

Among students who report experiencing physical harassment, six in 10 (57 percent) are harassed by one male. As with nonphysical harassment, this scenario is far more common for girls than for boys (84 percent vs. 25 percent).

Black boys are less likely than Hispanic or white boys to be physically harassed by one male (6 percent black vs. 15 percent Hispanic and 31 percent white). One-third (35 percent) of students are harassed by one female—again, more boys than girls (63 percent vs. 12 percent). (See Figure 16 on page 26 and Figure 17.)

Eight in 10 students who experience physical sexual harassment are harassed by a student (82 percent) and four in 10 are harassed by a former student (40 percent). Girls are more likely than boys to be harassed by a student (90 percent vs. 73 percent) or a former student (45 percent vs. 34 percent).

The statistic for physical harassment by a teacher mirrors that for nonphysical harassment: 7 percent of students, with boys and girls almost equally likely to have this experience (8 percent boys; 6 percent girls).

Where It Happens

Most harassment, nonphysical and physical, occurs in halls or classrooms for both boys and girls. Students most often report harassment in the following areas:

- The hall (71 percent for physical; 64 percent for nonphysical)

- A classroom (61 percent for physical; 56 percent for nonphysical)

WHY DIDN'T YOU TELL ANYONE?

Boys

- ❖ "I don't know. Thought it was normal kid stuff." (eighth-grader)

- ❖ "Because I didn't really care, it was not a big deal." (ninth-grader)

- ❖ "Because I'm a guy and I don't care. I'm not so insecure that someone saying I'm gay is gonna bother me. I'm not, so who cares?" (ninth-grader)

- ❖ "I could handle it myself." (11th-grader)

Girls

- ❖ "I don't know. I just didn't feel it necessary." (ninth-grader)

- ❖ "I liked it." (10th-grader)

- ❖ " ... make a mountain out of a molehill. I handled the situation myself, or they eventually went away." (10th-grader)

- ❖ "I didn't want to be a tattletale." (11th-grader)

- ❖ "It wasn't anything that bothered me, and I knew that it would stop. And it did." (11th-grader)

Figure 18
Where Were You Harassed (Nonphysical Harassment)?

	Total	Race/Ethnicity (Boys)			Race/Ethnicity (Girls)		
		White	Black	Hispanic	White	Black	Hispanic
Base:	1128	259	110	93	304	153	145
	%	%	%	%	%	%	%
In a classroom	56	50	48	42	65	59	53
In the hall	64	60	56	39	73	73	64
In the gym, playing field, or pool area	43	44	39	34	44	50	41
In the cafeteria	38	37	31	23	41	47	40
In the locker room area	21	32	12	19	15	17	18
In the restroom	12	18	6	13	7	9	15
In the parking lot	23	22	20	19	25	30	27
Outside the school, on school grounds (other than the parking lot)	42	40	37	30	43	58	39
On public transportation on the way to school or on the way home	17	15	19	14	14	29	24
On school transportation on the way to school, on the way home, or on a school trip	23	19	20	12	24	33	29
At a field trip location, including another school for away game	26	26	21	22	26	24	30
In the driver's education car	2	2	1	1	*	2	3

Base: In-school respondents who experienced nonphysical harassment

Figure 19
Where Were You Harassed (Physical Harassment)?

	Total	Race/Ethnicity (Boys)			Race/Ethnicity (Girls)		
		White	Black	Hispanic	White	Black	Hispanic
Base:	869	181	89	68	238	130	110
	%	%	%	%	%	%	%
In a classroom	61	57	47	50	69	69	53
In the hall	71	70	51	39	78	79	74
In the gym, playing field, or pool area	45	46	36	33	46	55	48
In the cafeteria	37	40	29	20	35	48	47
In the locker room area	20	30	12	16	12	19	23
In the restroom	12	16	7	15	7	16	17
In the parking lot	27	27	24	25	24	35	39
Outside the school, on school grounds (other than the parking lot)	41	40	36	31	42	54	45
On public transportation on the way to school or on the way home	17	18	16	17	9	37	23
On school transportation on the way to school, on the way home, or on a school trip	23	23	20	16	23	33	28
At a field trip location, including another school for away game	27	31	25	23	26	27	30
In the driver's education car	4	8	4	8	*	1	2

Base: In-school respondents who experienced physical harassment

Figure 20
Who Did You Tell (Nonphysical Harassment)?

	Total	Gender		Size of Place	
		Boys	Girls	Urban	Suburban/ Rural
Base:	1128	496	632	399	729
	%	%	%	%	%
A friend	61	45	75	63	60
A parent or family member	24	17	31	26	23
A teacher	11	7	14	12	10
A school employee (other than a teacher)	9	5	13	10	9
Someone else	23	19	27	25	22
No one	20	24	17	20	21

Base: In-school respondents who experienced nonphysical harassment

Figure 21
Who Did You Tell (Physical Harassment)?

	Total	Gender		Size of Place	
		Boys	Girls	Urban	Suburban/ Rural
Base:	1205	514	691	414	791
	%	%	%	%	%
A friend	67	53	78	66	67
A parent or family member	22	16	27	23	22
A teacher	11	7	15	10	12
A school employee (other than a teacher)	9	6	12	10	8
Someone else	27	22	31	24	28
No one	20	27	14	18	21

Base: In-school respondents who experienced physical harassment

- The gym, playing field, or pool area (45 percent for physical; 43 percent for nonphysical)

- Outside the school, on school grounds (other than the parking lot) (41 percent for physical; 42 percent for nonphysical)

- The cafeteria (37 percent for physical; 38 percent for nonphysical)

(See Figures 18 and 19 on page 28.) These areas are the most frequently reported locations of harassment in both urban and suburban/rural schools.

Race/ethnicity differentiates these findings. Black girls are more likely than white girls, for instance, to say they are harassed on public transportation to and from school and in the cafeteria. And white boys are twice as likely as Hispanic boys to be harassed in the cafeteria and locker room.

Danger zones differ for girls and boys. Girls are more likely than boys to experience nonphysical harassment in the classroom (62 percent vs. 49 percent) and hall (72 percent vs. 56 percent).

A higher percentage of boys experience nonphysical harassment in the locker room (28 percent vs. 15 percent) and restroom (15 percent vs. 9 percent).

The pattern is similar for physical sexual harassment. Sixty-six percent of girls compared to 54 percent of boys experience physical harassment in the classroom, and 77 percent of girls but only 63 percent of boys experience it in the halls. Twenty-six percent of boys compared to 15 percent of girls experience physical sexual harassment in the locker room.

Who Students Tell

Students are most likely to tell a friend if they are sexually harassed.

For nonphysical harassment, 61 percent tell a friend, 24 percent a relative, 11 percent a teacher, and 9 percent another school employee. Twenty percent tell no one. Boys are more likely than girls to tell no one (24 percent vs. 17 percent). (See Figure 20.)

Reports are similar for physical harassment: 67 percent of students tell a friend, 22 percent a relative, 11 percent a teacher, and 9 percent another school employee. Twenty percent tell no one. Again, boys are more likely than girls to tell no one (27 percent vs. 14 percent). (See Figure 21 on page 29.)

Students who tell someone about their experience of sexual harassment are most likely to receive the following reactions:

- Told to go to the authority and make them aware or tell parents (18 percent)

- Said it was a joke or laughed (13 percent)

- Said don't worry about it, it's not a big deal, forget about it (10 percent)

The highest percentage of boys say the people they told either laughed or thought it was a joke (21 percent), whereas the highest percentage of girls say they were told to report the incident (23 percent).

WHAT DID PEOPLE SAY WHEN YOU TOLD THEM?

Boys

❖ "Friends kind of laughed it off. Family was concerned enough to look into the matter." (ninth-grader)

❖ "Very little. Mostly, 'ask them to stop' or 'THAT'S NOT RIGHT!' kinds of things, neither of which tends to be particularly helpful. Or they laughed." (eighth-grader)

❖ "Don't worry about it, they are only joking." (10th-grader)

❖ "They blew me off and said they would 'speak to the principal.' Nothing ever became of it." (10th-grader)

❖ "They said that they would take action and get the person who offended me in serious trouble." (10th-grader)

❖ "Don't worry about it ... they're not serious." (11th-grader)

❖ "You just have to watch out for weird and disgusting people." (11th-grader)

❖ "Well my friends told me to tell a parent or teacher so I did and they took care of it." (11th-grader)

❖ "I know, she's a slut." (11th-grade boy)

Girls

❖ "The staff said that they would talk to the students involved." (eighth-grader)

❖ "Fight back." (eighth-grader)

❖ "They told me not to let them get to me. I really haven't been sexual harassed much. Maybe a few times and they were not very serious." (eighth-grader)

❖ "They say that I deserve it because of the way I dress and it makes them want to go after me." (eighth-grader)

❖ "Told me to report them to school officials." (10th-grader)

❖ "They were supportive and helpful, but didn't take any actions to prevent further situations." (10th-grader)

❖ "They were disgusted by a guy spreading a rumor about me." (11th-grader)

❖ "My friends shared their similar stories." (11th-grader)

❖ "My mom kept quiet about it, cause if my dad knew then he would go ballistic, and my friend did same thing, cause she know how bad my dad can get." (11th-grader)

Chapter 3:
The Impact

Many students accept harassment as just part of school life and not a big deal. Many others have a less sanguine attitude.

When asked about specific changes in their behavior or feelings as a result of their experiences, large numbers of students say sexual harassment upsets them and causes them to alter their lives or school routine. These negative repercussions to actual experiences may co-exist, for some students, with casual attitudes about harassment in general terms.

Nearly half (47 percent) of students say they are upset by occurrences of sexual harassment. Harassment affects students' school lives more tangibly as well. Some students, for instance, don't talk as much in class or don't want to go to school. Students who experience sexual harassment with physical contact, compared to nonphysical, are more likely to report these emotional and behavioral reactions.

Girls more than boys report feeling upset, ashamed, embarrassed, or self-conscious. Girls are also more likely to report specific educational repercussions, such as not wanting to go to school, trying to change seats or avoid particular students, not being able to pay attention in class, and not talking as much in class.

Emotional Impact

Nearly half (47 percent) of students who experience sexual harassment in school life feel very or somewhat upset right after the episode. (See Figure 22.)

In all, sexual harassment upsets 66 percent of girls compared to 28 percent of boys. Girls are more than twice as likely as boys to say they feel very upset (33 percent vs. 11 percent) or somewhat upset (33 percent vs. 17 percent). Boys are three times as likely as girls to say they aren't at all upset (23 percent vs. 7 percent). This reaction has not changed from 1993.

The type of harassment differentiates students' reactions. Both for girls and boys, physical harassment is twice as upsetting as nonphysical (56 percent vs. 26 percent).

Girls are far more likely than boys, however, to feel self-conscious (44 percent vs. 19 percent), embarrassed (53 percent vs. 32 percent), afraid (33 percent vs. 12 percent), or less self-assured or confident (32 percent vs. 16 percent) by physical or nonphysical harassment. (See Figure 23 on page 33.) Among boys, whites are more likely than blacks to feel self-conscious, embarrassed, or less self-assured or confident. (See Figure 24 on page 33.)

Students' feelings about their experience go beyond upset. Boys and girls describe their feelings in their own words:

- Bad, not good, yucky (10 percent)
- Angry, mad, annoyed (9 percent)
- Uncomfortable (9 percent)
- Hurt, upset, awful, disturbed (8 percent)
- Low self-esteem, worthless, useless (5 percent)
- Dirty, violated (4 percent)
- Scared, nervous, insecure (4 percent)

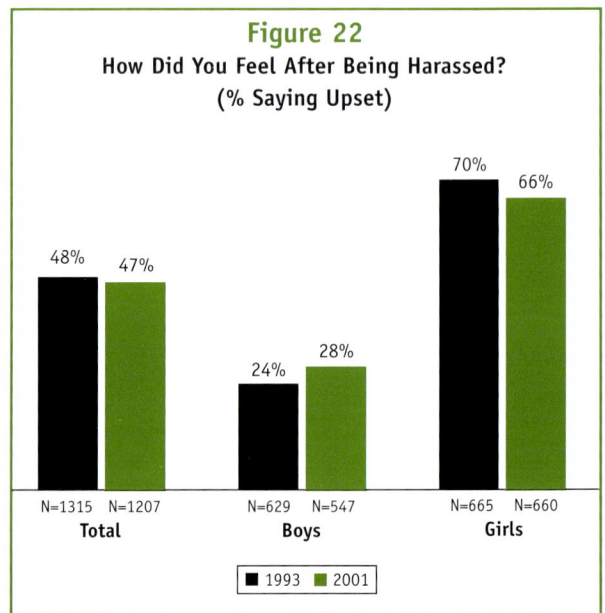

Figure 22
How Did You Feel After Being Harassed? (% Saying Upset)

Base: In-school respondents who experienced sexual harassment

Still, one-quarter (23 percent) of all students surveyed say they don't care, it's not a big deal, or they feel fine about the experience. As they do when asked the degree to which they are upset, boys more than girls say it's no big deal (30 percent vs. 17 percent). That is the reason, one-third (33 percent) of the boys explain, they don't tell anyone about their experiences with harassment. Only 10 percent of girls offer this reason for not telling.

Students report these emotional reactions to sexual harassment:

- Four in 10 students (43 percent) feel embarrassed

- One-third (32 percent) of students feel self-conscious

- One-quarter (24 percent) feel less sure of themselves or less confident

- One-quarter (23 percent) feel afraid or scared

Girls are more likely than boys to say they experience most of these feelings after being sexually harassed. Eighth- and ninth-graders are more likely than 10th- and 11th-graders to feel afraid or scared (27 percent vs. 18 percent). White students are more likely than blacks to feel embarrassed (35 percent white vs. 14 percent black boys; 57 percent white vs. 31 percent black girls).

Figure 23
What Was the Emotional Impact?

	Total	Gender		Grade	
		Boys	Girls	8-9	10-11
Base:	1207	547	660	517	690
	%	%	%	%	%
Feel self-conscious	32	19	44	32	32
Feel embarrassed	43	32	53	44	41
Feel afraid or scared	23	12	33	27	18
Be less sure of yourself or less confident	24	16	32	24	23
Feel confused about who you are	17	12	22	18	15
Doubt whether you have what it takes to graduate from high school	5	4	7	7	3
Doubt whether you have what it takes to continue your education after high school	6	5	6	7	4
Doubt whether you can have a happy romantic relationship	19	12	25	20	16

Base: In-school respondents who experienced sexual harassment

Figure 24
What Was the Emotional Impact (by Race/Ethnicity and Gender)?

	Total	Race/Ethnicity (Boys)			Race/Ethnicity (Girls)		
		White	Black	Hispanic	White	Black	Hispanic
Base:	1207	278	124	105	313	163	153
	%	%	%	%	%	%	%
Feel self-conscious	32	21	8	15	49	25	43
Feel embarrassed	43	35	14	25	57	31	52
Feel afraid or scared	23	13	4	13	33	26	34
Be less sure of yourself or less confident	24	17	4	12	35	17	31
Feel confused about who you are	17	12	2	14	21	21	27
Doubt whether you have what it takes to graduate from high school	5	3	1	6	6	2	11
Doubt whether you have what it takes to continue your education after high school	6	5	*	9	6	3	8
Doubt whether you can have a happy romantic relationship	19	12	5	9	25	23	27

Base: In-school respondents who experienced sexual harassment

Figure 25
What Was the Emotional Impact?

Emotional Impact	Experienced Physical Harassment (N=869)	Experienced Nonphysical Harassment (N=300)
Feel self-conscious	38%	17%
Feel embarrassed	48%	29%
Feel afraid or scared	28%	10%
Be less sure of yourself or less confident	28%	13%
Feel confused about who you are	21%	5%
Doubt whether you have what it takes to graduate from high school	6%	2%
Doubt whether you have what it takes to continue your education after high school	7%	2%
Doubt whether you can have a happy romantic relationship	23%	6%

■ Experienced Physical Harassment (N=869)   ■ Experienced Nonphysical Harassment (N=300)

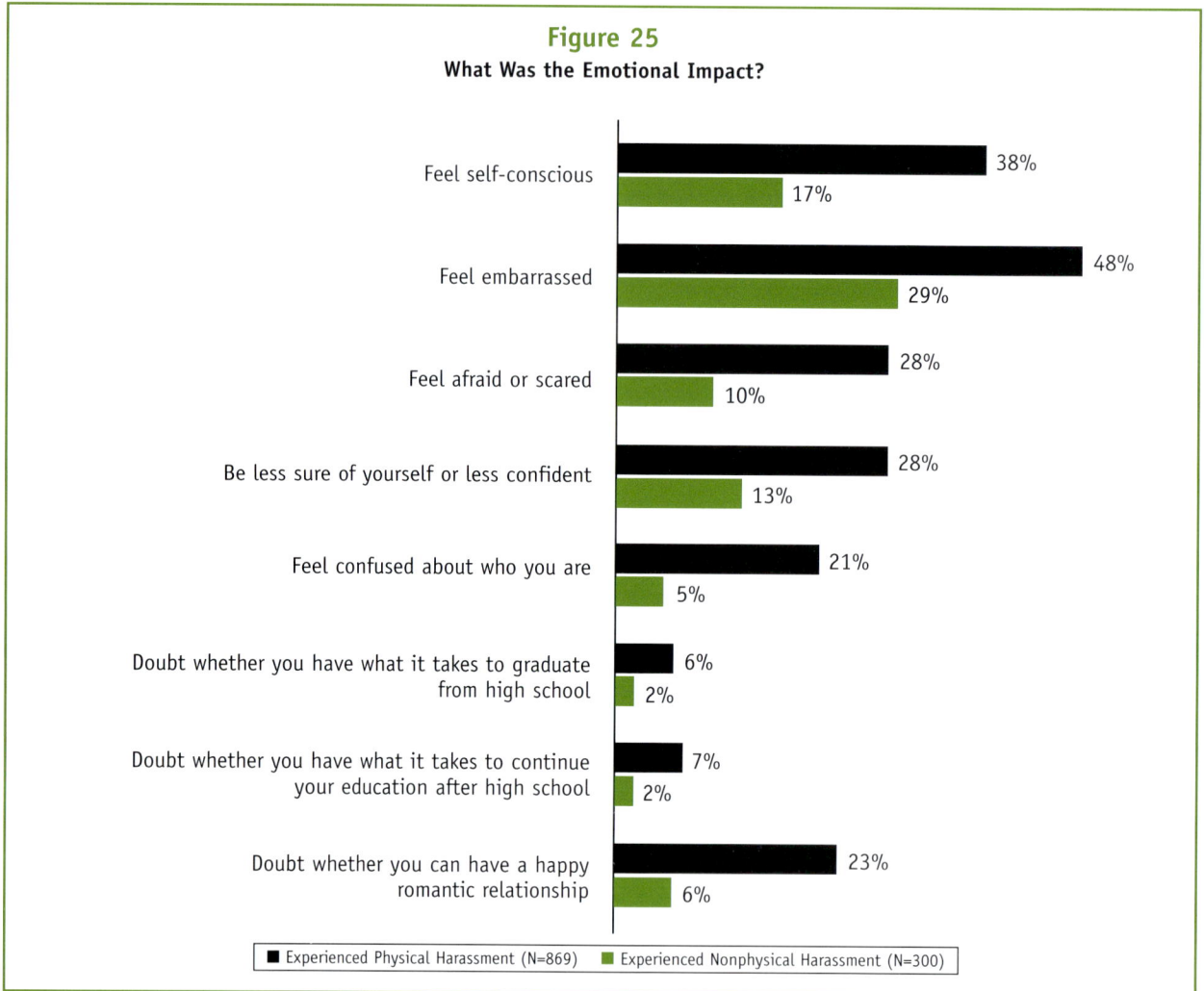

Base: In-school respondents who experienced sexual harassment

As seen previously among students who actually experience harassment, physical harassment hurts more than nonphysical. (See Figure 25.) Students who experience physical harassment are more likely to experience the following consequences:

■ Feel embarrassed (48 percent vs. 29 percent)

■ Feel self-conscious (38 percent vs. 17 percent)

■ Be less sure of themselves or less confident (28 percent vs. 13 percent)

■ Feel afraid or scared (28 percent vs. 10 percent)

■ Doubt whether they can have a happy romantic relationship (23 percent vs. 6 percent)

■ Feel confused about who they are (21 percent vs. 5 percent)

When asked in open-ended questions to describe their reactions to personal experiences with harassment, boys and girls respond somewhat differently.

Many boys confuse sexual harassment with positive sexual attention and say they are flattered by the experience. "Not too bad," responds one 11th-grade boy. "I like just about all sexual contact." A 10th-grade boy says his reaction "depends on whether it's a fine or beautiful girl and what the situation is."

Many other boys respond that the sexual harassment isn't a big deal, especially insofar as it occurred in the context of joking among friends. Some answers reveal widespread, casual homophobia in schools. "It was just a joke," a ninth-grade boy writes, "and you just call him a fag back and move

on with your life." An eighth-grade boy writes, "If it's a girl I really don't mind but if it's a guy I really care." A smaller number of boys do report feeling angry, upset, or "like an outsider." One 11th-grade boy says it makes him feel "a little angry, but not enough to report it to an authority figure."

Several girls say they distinguish between teasing and joking and more disturbing events, particularly

HOW DID THE HARASSMENT MAKE YOU FEEL?

Boys

- ❖ "Disturbed and generally angry." (eighth-grader)

- ❖ "Good." (eighth-grader)

- ❖ "Mad and upset." (ninth-grader)

- ❖ "It was just a joke, and you can just call him fag back and move on with your life." (ninth-grader)

- ❖ "They don't bother me much, because they don't happen often and I feel that I have good self-esteem and deal with things well, but I don't feel good in any way when they do occur." (ninth-grader)

- ❖ "I guess uncomfortable, of course. It's not fun for anyone to get harassed." (ninth-grader)

- ❖ "Like people can't have innocent fun anymore because it is subject to being harassment." (ninth-grader)

- ❖ "Kinda grossed out." (10th-grader)

- ❖ "It bugged me, but I blew it off ... they're just idiots." (10th-grader)

- ❖ "The girl was very attractive and I was not upset at all." (10th-grader)

- ❖ "Surprised." (11th-grader)

Girls

- ❖ "I was very upset. I cried for someone even thinking that, but I had my friends to help me." (eighth-grader)

- ❖ "Not very upset." (eighth-grader)

- ❖ "Angry, embarrassed, hurt feelings." (eighth-grader)

- ❖ "They make me feel like I don't belong with this people and I am too mature for them." (eighth-grader)

- ❖ "I didn't care. It's a joke." (ninth-grader)

- ❖ "Like guys like me!" (ninth-grader)

- ❖ "Like I have lost most of my respect for the male gender." (10th-grader)

- ❖ "Somewhat fine, to have the attention, but then after that was over, I felt kinda weird about it." (10th-grader)

- ❖ "I just brush these things off because boys will be boys unless they harm me or I feel I have been violated in anyway." (10th-grader)

- ❖ "Uncomfortable and uneasy." (11th-grader)

- ❖ "It doesn't really bother me because it has only happened a couple of times, and it has happened to my friends too. It wasn't a big deal, like rape or something." (11th-grader)

"[It made me feel] sort of sick to my stomach, but a little aroused at the same time. I sort of felt dirty afterward though, because I didn't completely condemn what they were doing. I just let them do it."

—ninth-grade girl

if they can discern the intention or mood of the other student. "It was fun because they were only fooling around and it wasn't serious," one 10th-grade girl responds. "It doesn't bother me that much," writes another 10th-grade girl. "[It] probably would more if it involved adults or older people. The only time it really bothers me when my peers do it is if I'm in a bitchy mood and I don't like the person that much anyway."

Unlike boys, however, only a handful of girls report any positive feelings—such as flattery or arousal—associated with these experiences. Girls are more likely in open-ended questions, as evident in other questions on the survey, to describe a much broader range of negative reactions and feelings.

A sizeable number of girls reports that sexual harassment makes them feel ashamed of themselves, "dirty-like a piece of trash," "terrible," "awkward," "uncomfortable," "grossed out," "scared," "embarrassed," "angry and upset," and "like a second-class citizen."

"I was very upset," an eighth-grade girl writes. "I cried for someone even thinking that, but I had my friends to help me." Says an eighth-grade girl, "They made me feel not good enough to date anyone—it makes me feel slutty." A 10th-grade girl feels "annoyed" by harassment, "especially ... when no one objects, including other females."

Behavioral Impact

Experiencing school sexual harassment has behavioral as well as emotional consequences. (See Figure 26 on page 37 and Figure 27 on page 38.) Students list these most common changes in their lives:

- Avoiding the person who bothered or harassed them (40 percent)

- Not talking as much in class (24 percent)

- Not wanting to go to school (22 percent)

- Changing their seat in class to get farther away from someone (21 percent)

- Finding it hard to pay attention in school (20 percent)

- Staying away from particular places in the school or on the school grounds (18 percent)

- Finding it hard to study (16 percent)

- Losing their appetite or not being interested in eating (16 percent)

- Staying home from school or cutting a class (16 percent)

Overall, girls are more likely than boys to report these types of consequences. Girls and boys also differ somewhat in terms of their reactions. For girls, the most frequent responses are to avoid the person who bothered or harassed them (56 percent), change their seat in class to get farther away from someone (31 percent), not talk as much in class (30 percent), and not want to go to school (30 percent). Boys, on the other hand, are most likely to avoid the person who bothered or harassed them (24 percent), not talk as much in class (18 percent), not want to go to school (15 percent), and find it hard to pay attention in school (15 percent).

As with students' emotional responses, physical harassment causes more reactions than nonphysical. Most notably, students who experience physical sexual harassment are more than twice as likely to say they react by avoiding the person who bothered or harassed them (48 percent vs. 20 percent). They are also more likely to say that physical harassment, compared to nonphysical, causes them to do the following:

- Not talk as much in class (28 percent vs. 14 percent)

- Not want to go to school (27 percent vs. 12 percent)

- Change their seat in class to get farther away from someone (25 percent vs. 11 percent)

- Find it hard to pay attention in school (25 percent vs. 7 percent)

- Stay away from particular places in the school or on the school grounds (22 percent vs. 9 percent)

- Find it hard to study (19 percent vs. 10 percent)

- Lose their appetite or not be interested in eating (19 percent vs. 7 percent)

- Stay home from school or cut a class (19 percent vs. 7 percent)

- Have trouble sleeping (17 percent vs. 8 percent)

- Get someone to protect you (16 percent vs. 3 percent)

- Make a lower grade on a test or paper than they think they otherwise would have (15 percent vs. 8 percent)

- Make a lower grade in a class than you think you otherwise would have (14 percent vs. 5 percent)

Figure 26
What Was the Behavioral Impact?

| | Total | Gender | | Grade | |
		Boys	Girls	8-9	10-11
Base:	1207	547	660	517	690
	%	%	%	%	%
Have trouble sleeping	14	9	20	14	14
Lose your appetite/not be interested in eating	16	8	23	17	15
Not want to go to school	22	15	30	25	19
Stay home from school or cut a class	16	10	22	16	15
Not talk as much in class	24	18	30	25	23
Stop attending a particular activity or sport	9	7	10	9	8
Find it hard to pay attention in school	20	15	24	23	16
Change your group of friends	10	9	12	10	11
Drop out of a course	3	3	4	3	4
Change the way you come to or go home from school	9	6	12	10	8
Change your seat in class to get farther away from someone	21	10	31	22	20
Think about changing schools	10	7	13	12	8
Change schools	4	4	4	3	5
Get into trouble with school authorities	7	7	7	7	7
Get someone to protect you	12	5	18	14	10
Find it hard to study	16	13	20	20	12
Make a lower grade on a test or paper than you think you otherwise would have	13	10	16	16	10
Make a lower grade in a class than you think you otherwise would have	11	8	14	13	9
Stay away from particular places in the school or on the school grounds	18	11	25	21	15
Avoid the person that bothered/harassed you in any other way	40	24	56	42	38

Base: In-school respondents who experienced sexual harassment

■ Change their group of friends (12 percent vs. 5 percent)

■ Think about changing schools (12 percent vs. 3 percent)

■ Change the way they come to or go home from school (11 percent vs. 4 percent)

■ Stop attending a particular activity or sport (10 percent vs. 3 percent)

Figure 27
What Was the Behavioral Impact (by Race/Ethnicity and Gender)?

	Total	Race/Ethnicity (Boys)			Race/Ethnicity (Girls)		
		White	Black	Hispanic	White	Black	Hispanic
Base:	1207	278	124	105	313	163	153
	%	%	%	%	%	%	%
Have trouble sleeping	14	8	5	9	20	15	22
Lose your appetite/not be interested in eating	16	7	6	11	24	17	25
Not want to go to school	22	15	6	15	32	21	27
Stay home from school or cut a class	16	9	1	10	21	17	24
Not talk as much in class	24	16	14	14	31	26	27
Stop attending a particular activity or sport	9	7	5	9	9	10	12
Find it hard to pay attention in school	20	14	13	11	24	14	31
Change your group of friends	10	9	7	12	11	21	8
Drop out of a course	3	3	1	6	4	3	3
Change the way you come to or go home from school	9	5	3	14	9	14	22
Change your seat in a class to get farther away from someone	21	9	7	18	32	32	29
Think about changing schools	10	6	4	10	12	14	14
Change schools	4	4	-	4	3	3	3
Get into trouble with school authorities	7	6	5	7	5	10	8
Get someone to protect you	12	5	4	10	17	17	22
Find it hard to study	16	11	5	13	18	9	28
Make a lower grade on a test or paper than you think you otherwise would have	13	9	2	7	16	11	19
Make a lower grade in a class than you think you otherwise would have	11	7	2	9	13	11	19
Stay away from particular places in the school or on the school grounds	18	12	4	13	22	26	35
Avoid the person that bothered/harassed you in any other way	40	23	16	26	57	52	52

Base: In-school respondents who experienced sexual harassment

Chapter 4:
Students Who Harass

lightly fewer students today than in 1993 say they ever sexually harassed someone else at school. In addition, younger students are more likely than older students to say this. These survey findings prompt several questions: Have research on sexual harassment and attempts to address the behavior resulted in positive changes? Does age sensitize students' actual behavior? Or are these changes caused by students' concerns about reporting inappropriate behavior?

Students as Perpetrators

Today, 54 percent of students admit to harassing someone in their school lives, down from 59 percent in 1993. This change is mostly attributable to the drop in boys' admissions, down from 66 percent in 1993 to 57 percent today. (See Figure 28.)

Still, though, boys are more likely than girls to be perpetrators, whether often, occasionally, or rarely (57 percent vs. 50 percent) or often or occasionally (33 percent vs. 21 percent).

Ways That Students Harass

In particular, substantial percentages of students—generally boys more than girls—report harassing someone in these ways:

- Making sexual comments, jokes, gestures, or looks (48 percent boys vs. 36 percent girls)
- Calling someone gay or lesbian (38 percent boys vs. 29 percent girls)
- Touching, grabbing, or pinching someone in a sexual way (28 percent boys vs. 22 percent girls)
- Intentionally brushing up against someone in a sexual way (26 percent boys vs. 18 percent girls)
- Flashing or "mooning" someone (22 percent boys vs. 15 percent girls)
- Spreading sexual rumors about someone (19 percent boys vs. 14 percent girls)

- Showing, giving, or leaving someone sexual pictures, photographs, illustrations, messages, or notes (19 percent boys vs. 10 percent girls)
- Pulling at someone's clothing in a sexual way (17 percent boys vs. 10 percent girls)
- Blocking someone's way or cornering someone in a sexual way (13 percent boys vs. 7 percent girls)

Some of these findings differ by race/ethnicity. White boys are more likely than Hispanic and black boys to call someone gay or lesbian (40 percent white vs. 33 percent Hispanic and 29 percent black) or spread sexual rumors (21 percent white vs. 14 percent Hispanic and 16 percent black). Black boys are more likely than Hispanic and white boys to touch, grab, or pinch someone in a sexual way (35 percent black vs. 24 percent Hispanic and 28 percent white) or intentionally brush up against someone in a sexual way (34 percent black vs. 19 percent Hispanic and 26 percent white).

Some findings also differ by grade level, particularly among girls. While 58 percent of eighth- and ninth-graders say they ever harassed someone at school, that figure drops to 48 percent for 10th- and 11th-

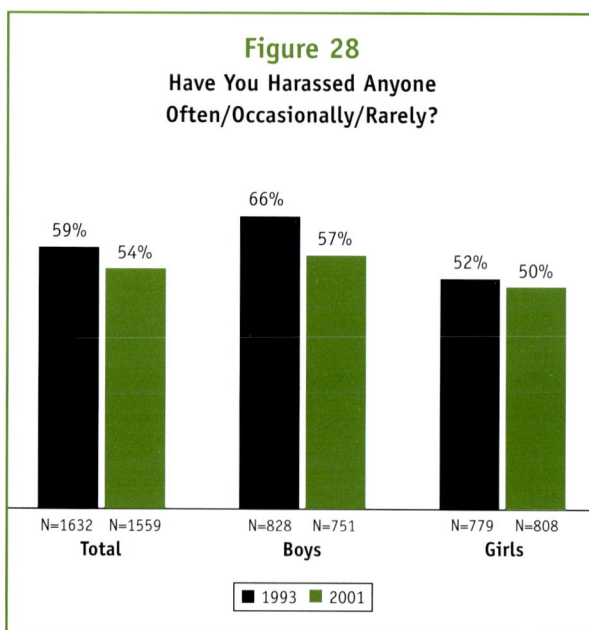

Figure 28
Have You Harassed Anyone Often/Occasionally/Rarely?

	Total	Boys	Girls
1993	59%	66%	52%
2001	54%	57%	50%
N (1993)	1632	828	779
N (2001)	1559	751	808

Base: In-school respondents

graders. In eighth and ninth grades, the gender gap is 60 percent boys vs. 57 percent girls; in grades 10 and 11, the gap widens to 54 percent boys vs. 42 percent girls.

Victims of Harassment

Half (51 percent) of students who report sexually harassing someone say they harassed a student of the other sex. In contrast, 16 percent say they harassed a student of the same sex, while only 4 percent say they harassed a teacher or other school employee.

Black boys are more likely than white or Hispanic boys to say the victim was a girl (70 percent black vs. 52 percent white and 46 percent Hispanic). White boys are more likely than black or Hispanic boys to say the victim was another boy (24 percent vs. 5 percent and 17 percent). The survey findings show no such racial/ethnic differences among girls.

Why Students Harass

Students who harass provide several reasons. (See Figure 29.)

- Four in 10 (39 percent) say it's just part of school life, a lot of people do it, or it's no big deal.

- Three in 10 (28 percent) say they thought the person liked it.

- One-quarter (26 percent) say they wanted a date with that person.

- One-quarter (24 percent) say their friends encouraged or pushed them to do it.

Figure 29
Why Did You Sexually Harass Someone?

| | Total | Gender | |
		Boys	Girls
Base:	804	418	386
	%	%	%
It's just part of school life/ a lot of people do it/ it's no big deal	39	43	34
I wanted that person to think that I had some sort of power over them	11	10	12
I wanted something from that person	17	18	16
My friends encouraged me/ "pushed" me into doing it	24	23	24
I thought the person liked it	28	29	26
I wanted a date with that person	26	27	24

Base: In-school respondents who sexually harassed someone

Afterword From AAUW

In some ways, the data from this study present a somewhat paradoxical picture of boys' and girls' interactions in school.

When Harris first conducted this survey for the AAUW Educational Foundation in 1993, students had little awareness of school policies or procedures related to sexual harassment, although the *experience* of harassment was nearly universal. The good news today is students' increased awareness of their schools' harassment policies and materials. The bad news is that this increased awareness has not translated into fewer incidents of sexual harassment in school life.

Disturbingly, reports of harassment remain high: Eight students in 10 report that they experience sexual harassment; one student in four experiences it often. And while students are aware of their schools' sexual harassment policies and procedures, neither girls nor boys are likely to report actual incidents to adults.

Students' reactions are likewise paradoxical. On the one hand, some students are resigned to sexual teasing and harassment. "It's just a part of school life," they say. "It's no big deal." On the other hand, many students say it makes them feel "dirty" and "violated" and causes them to change their seats, avoid particular places, or not talk as much in class. Students may project a tough response to the social trials of school life, and even coarsen their own behavior to combat it. But both girls and boys find the incidents troubling and distressing.

Recommendations

The Foundation applauds schools' sexual harassment policies and procedures, which can promote students' emotional and educational well-being. The next step is for parents, educators, and activists to focus on changing the culture of harassment in schools and promoting students' use of existing resources to address the problem.

For example, students may resist discussing an incident with adults because they don't want to be seen as a snitch or they fear repercussions would be too extreme. Are there ways to encourage students to discuss interpersonal problems before they escalate into crises? What programs in schools and classrooms spur changes in behavior and not just in policy?

Many AAUW branches have taken the lead in dealing with sexual harassment in school. Through Sister-to-Sister Summits, girls bring the problem to light and brainstorm strategies to help them confront it. Some AAUW branches have also engaged boys in the dialogue through Sister-to-Brother Summits, aimed at getting girls and boys to talk about how they perceive one another, why they may misunderstand each other, and how they can move toward solving their own conflicts in school. Other branches have coordinated workshops on sexual harassment and bullying.

Through activities such as these, girls and boys themselves might transform the culture of fear and harassment to a culture of camaraderie and trust.

Appendix: Methodology

For this report, Harris Interactive surveyed a nationally representative sample of 2,064 public school students in grades eight through 11. Students were surveyed using a self-administered questionnaire either during an English class or online.

School Survey

A total of 1,559 public school students in grades eight through 11 were surveyed during an English class using a self-administered questionnaire. Interviews averaged 38 minutes and were conducted between Sept. 7 and Nov. 22, 2000.

Harris Interactive's national probability sample of schools and students is based on a highly stratified two-stage sampling design. This design employs features similar to the sample designs used in various national surveys of students and schools conducted by the U.S. National Center of Education Statistics. A sample was drawn from a list of approximately 80,000 public, private, and parochial schools in the United States. The sample was selected to account for differences in grade enrollment, region, and the size of the municipality in which the schools are located. A random selection of schools was drawn on the basis of the number of students in each cell proportionate to the number of students in the universe, creating a cross section of young people in a set of designated grades. For this study, only public schools were selected. An eligible grade was randomly assigned to each school.

Harris Interactive then sent a letter to principals soliciting their participation and followed up with a phone call. If the principal agreed to participate, Harris employed a random selection process to choose a particular class to complete the survey. The principal alphabetized all classes for the grade assigned by Harris. Using a random number selection grid, an interviewer identified an individual class. For junior and senior high school, where students attend different classes for each subject, only English classes were selected. Since all students in

all grades must study English, this ensured a more representative sample of students by academic track and level of achievement.

Harris included a number of steps in the consent process to maximize response rates. The alert letter contained a brief description of the survey process and information on Harris. A letter from the AAUW Educational Foundation described its involvement in and the importance of this research. A copy of the questionnaire was included in the packet. Schools were also offered an incentive to participate. In addition, at a principal's request, Harris called local school boards or district offices to gain approval from the appropriate officials. If necessary, Harris faxed or mailed copies of the introductory letters and other materials to the principal and other school officials. By surveying only one class in each school, Harris imposed on the schools as little as possible.

To preserve the integrity of the primary selection, a school that could not participate was replaced by a school with similar demographic characteristics. Another randomly drawn school was chosen within the same region, with similar grade enrollment and size of municipality, and in the same or the nearest zip code to the original school.

To administer the test, in each class a trained interviewer from Harris distributed questionnaires and provided instruction to the students. Due to the sensitive nature of the questions, teachers were asked to either leave the room or sit at the front. In addition, teachers received a bibliography of resources concerning sexual harassment in schools and surveys. By providing these educational materials, including *The Basic Primer on Public Opinion Polling*, Harris hoped teachers would weave this exercise into the classroom curriculum in a meaningful way. Finally, students were given envelopes in which to seal their completed surveys before returning them to the interviewer. The survey instrument is anonymous; at no point were students asked to provide their names.

After survey completion, Harris Interactive carefully edited and checked all surveys for completeness and accuracy. Surveys with significant errors or large proportions of missing data were removed from the batch; typically this represented less than 1 percent of the questionnaires collected. As with all self-administered questionnaires, however, occasional questions were sometimes left blank. Findings for each question are reported based on the total number of potential respondents in the sample. As an overall check, each questionnaire was reviewed to ensure that a majority of all possible responses had been completed.

Online Survey

The survey questionnaire was self-administered online by means of the Internet to 505 public school students in grades eight through 11 who have access to the Internet. Interviews averaged 15 minutes and were conducted between Sept. 28 and Oct. 11, 2000.

A sample was drawn from the Harris Poll Online database of approximately 6.5 million households who are registered as participants. To reach students in grades eight through 11, the sample was drawn from the Youth Panel, a subset of the Harris Interactive Panel of Cooperative Respondents. This subset currently has nearly 500,000 members under age 18.

Harris obtains e-mail addresses for households in the database from participation in the following sources: Youth Panel web communities (HarrisZone.com and HarrisKidZone.com), Harris Poll Online registration, the Harris/Excite Poll, Harris Poll Online banner advertisements, Excite and Netscape product registrations, Harris telephone research, media recruitment, and sweepstakes sponsored by Matchlogic and its subsidiaries (such as DeliverE and Preferences.com). Invitations for this study were e-mailed to a selected sample of the database identified as being 13 to 20 years old and residing in the United States.

Interviews were conducted using a self-administered, online questionnaire via Harris' proprietary, web-assisted interviewing software. The Harris Online interviewing system permits respondents to enter interview data online. Questionnaires are programmed into the system with the following checks:

1. Question and response series

2. Skip patterns

3. Question rotation

4. Range checks

5. Mathematical checks

6. Consistency checks

7. Special edit procedures

For questions with precoded responses, the system only permits answers within a specified range. If, for example, a question had three possible answer choices (e.g., agree, disagree, not sure), the system only accepted coded responses corresponding to these choices. All data was tabulated, checked for internal consistency, and processed by computer. The computer then generated a series of tables for each sample group showing the results of each survey question, both by the total number of respondents and by important subgroups.

To maintain the reliability and integrity in the sample, the following procedures were used:

1. Password protection: Each invitation contained a password uniquely assigned to that e-mail address. A respondent was required to enter the password at the beginning of the survey to gain access into the survey. Password protection ensured that a respondent completed the survey only one time.

2. Reminder invitations: To increase the number of respondents in the survey and to improve overall response rates, Harris Interactive mailed people who had not yet participated in the survey up to two additional reminder invitations at two- to four-day intervals.

3. Summary of the survey findings: To increase the number of respondents in the survey and to improve overall response rates, respondents were often provided with a summary of some of the survey responses. Respondents were sent an e-mail that gave them access to a website containing the survey findings to date. As with the survey itself, the website was password-protected and accessible for only a limited period (one to two weeks).

The data-processing staff performed machine edits and additional cleaning for the entire data set. The edit programs acted as a verification of the skip instructions and other data checks written into the online program. The edit programs listed any errors by case number, question number, and type. Senior electronic data-processing personnel then inspected the original file and made appropriate corrections. Complete records were kept of all such procedures.

type of survey. The chances are 95 in 100 that the survey results do not vary, plus or minus, by more than the indicated number of percentage points from the results that would have been obtained had interviews been conducted with all persons in the universe represented by the sample.

For example, if the response for a sample size of 300 were 30 percent, then in 95 out of 100 cases the response of the total population would be between 25 percent and 35 percent.

Survey results based on subgroups of a small size can be subject to large sampling error.

Sampling tolerances also are involved when comparing results from different parts of the sample (subgroup analysis) or from different surveys. Figure A.2 on page 49 shows the percentage difference that must be obtained before a difference can

Weighting of Student Data

Data were weighted to reflect the national population of public school students in grades eight through 11 for key demographic variables: grade, gender, race/ethnicity, and region. Demographic weights were based on data from the U.S. National Center of Education Statistics. In addition, data collected online were weighted to key behavioral and attitudinal variables to align it with the data collected using the school methodology.

Reliability of Survey Percentages

The results from any survey sample are subject to sampling variation. The magnitude of this variation is measurable and is affected by both the number of interviews involved and the level of the percentages expressed in the results.

Figure A.1 shows the range of sampling variation that applies to percentage results for this

Figure A.1
Approximate Sampling Tolerances (at 95 Percent Confidence) to Use in Evaluating Percentage Results

Number of People Asked Question on Which Survey Result is Based	Survey Percentage Result at 10 or 90 Percent	Survey Percentage Result at 20 or 80 Percent	Survey Percentage Result at 30 or 70 Percent	Survey Percentage Result at 40 or 60 Percent	Survey Percentage Result at 50 Percent
2,000	1	2	2	2	2
1,500	2	2	2	2	3
1,000	2	2	3	3	3
900	2	3	3	3	3
800	2	3	3	3	3
700	2	3	3	4	4
600	2	3	4	4	4
500	3	4	4	4	4
400	3	4	4	5	5
300	3	5	5	6	6
200	4	6	6	7	7
100	6	8	9	10	10
50	8	11	13	14	14

be considered statistically significant. These figures too represent the 95 percent confidence interval.

For example, suppose 34 percent of one group of 1,000 and 28 percent of an independent group of 500 responds "yes" to the same question, for an observed difference of 6 percentage points. According to Figure A.2, this difference is subject to a potential sampling error of 5 percentage points. Since the observed difference is greater than the sampling error, the observed difference is considered statistically significant.

Non-Sampling Error

Sampling error is only one way in which survey findings may vary from the findings that would result from interviewing every member of the relevant population. Survey research is susceptible to human and mechanical errors as well, such as errors in handling data and interviewer recording. The procedures used by Harris, including the computer-assisted interviewing systems described earlier, keep these types of errors to a minimum.

Figure A.2
Approximate Sampling Tolerances (at 95 Percent Confidence) to Use in Evaluating Differences Between Two Percentage Results

Approximate Sample Size of Two Groups Asked Question on Which Survey Result is Based	Survey Percentage Result at 10 or 90 Percent	Survey Percentage Result at 20 or 80 Percent	Survey Percentage Result at 30 or 70 Percent	Survey Percentage Result at 40 or 60 Percent	Survey Percentage Result at 50 Percent
5,000 vs. 2,000	2	2	2	3	3
1,000	2	3	3	3	3
500	3	4	4	5	5
300	3	5	5	6	6
200	4	6	6	7	7
100	6	8	9	10	10
50	8	11	13	14	14
2,000 vs. 2,000	2	2	3	3	3
1,000	2	3	3	4	4
500	3	4	4	5	5
200	4	6	7	7	7
100	6	8	9	10	10
50	8	11	13	14	14
1,000 vs. 1,000	3	4	4	4	4
500	3	4	5	5	5
200	5	6	7	7	8
100	6	8	9	10	10
50	9	11	13	14	14
500 vs. 500	4	5	6	6	6
200	5	7	8	8	8
100	6	9	10	11	11
50	9	12	13	14	15
200 vs. 200	6	8	9	10	10
100	7	10	11	12	12
50	9	12	14	15	15
100 vs. 100	8	11	13	14	14
50	10	14	16	17	17
50 vs. 50	12	16	18	19	20

AAUW
Equity Library

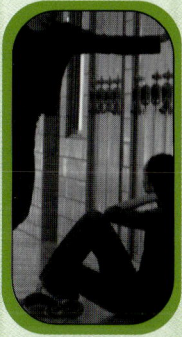

Hostile Hallways: Bullying, Teasing, and Sexual Harassment in School

One student in five fears being hurt or bothered in school; four students in five personally experience sexual harassment. These are among the findings of this nationally representative survey of 2,064 eighth- through 11th-graders. The report investigates sexual harassment in public schools, comparing the findings with AAUW's original survey in 1993 and exploring differences in responses by gender, race/ethnicity, grade level, and area (urban or suburban/rural). Conducted by Harris Interactive. 56 pages/2001.
$8.95 AAUW members/$9.95 nonmembers.

Beyond the "Gender Wars": A Conversation About Girls, Boys, and Education

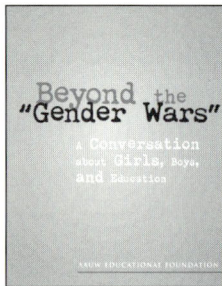

Report of the key insights presented during a symposium convened by the AAUW Educational Foundation in September 2000 to foster a discussion among scholars who study both girls' and boys' experiences in and out of school. Participants share their insights about gender identity and difference, challenge popular views of girls' and boys' behavior, and explore the meaning of equitable education for the 21st century. 60 pages/2001.
$8.95 AAUW members/$9.95 nonmembers.

¡Sí, Se Puede! Yes, We Can: Latinas in School

by Angela Ginorio and Michelle Huston

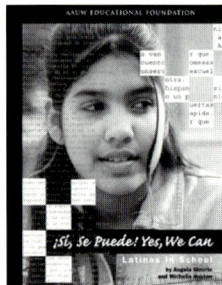

Comprehensive look at the status of Latina girls in the U.S. public education system. Report explores conflicts between institutional expectations and the realities of student lives and discusses the social, cultural, and community factors that affect Hispanic education. Available in English and Spanish. 84 pages/2001.
$11.95 AAUW members/$12.95 nonmembers.

A License for Bias: Sex Discrimination, Schools, and Title IX

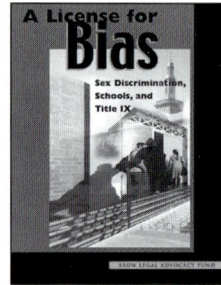

Examines uneven efforts to implement the 1972 civil rights law that protects some 70 million students and employees from sex discrimination in schools and universities. The analysis of non-sports-related complaints filed between 1993 and 1997 pinpoints problems that hamper enforcement and includes recommendations for Congress, the Office for Civil Rights, and educational institutions. 84 pages/2000.
$11.95 AAUW members/$12.95 nonmembers. Published by the AAUW Legal Advocacy Fund.

Community Coalitions Manual With Lessons Learned From the Girls Can! Project

A comprehensive guide for establishing and sustaining effective coalition-based programs. Covers volunteer recruitment, project planning, evaluation, fundraising, and public relations, with contact information for more than 200 organizations, and lessons learned from the Girls Can! Community Coalitions Projects, a nationwide gender equity program. 172 pages/2000.
$14.95 AAUW members/$16.95 nonmembers.

Tech-Savvy: Educating Girls in the New Computer Age

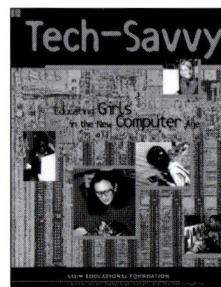

Explores girls' and teachers' perspectives of today's computer culture and technology use at school, home, and the workplace. Presents recommendations for broadening access to computers for girls and others who don't fit the "male hacker/computer geek" stereotype. 84 pages/2000.
$11.95 AAUW members/$12.95 nonmembers.

Voices of a Generation: Teenage Girls on Sex, School, and Self

Compares the comments of roughly 2,100 girls nationwide on peer pressure, sexuality, the media, and school. The girls participated in AAUW teen forums called Sister-to-Sister Summits. The report explores differences in responses by race, ethnicity, and age and offers action proposals to solve common problems. 95 pages/1999.
$13.95 AAUW members/$14.95 nonmembers.

Gaining a Foothold: Women's Transitions Through Work and College

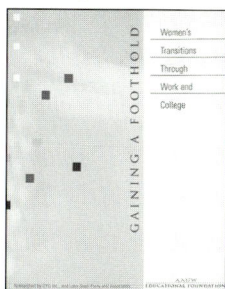

Examines how and why women make changes in their lives through education. The report profiles three groups—women going from high school to college, from high school to work, and from work back to formal education—using both quantitative and qualitative methods. Report findings include an analysis of women's educational decisions, aspirations, and barriers. 100 pages/1999.
$11.95 AAUW members/$12.95 nonmembers.

Gender Gaps: Where Schools Still Fail Our Children

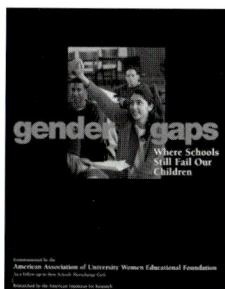

Measures schools' mixed progress toward gender equity and excellence since the 1992 publication of *How Schools Shortchange Girls: The AAUW Report*. Research compares student course enrollments, tests, grades, risks, and resiliency by race and class as well as gender. It finds some gains in girls' achievement, some areas where boys—not girls—lag, and some areas, like technology, where needs have not yet been addressed. 150 pages/1998.
$12.95 AAUW members/$13.95 nonmembers.

Gender Gaps Executive Summary

Overview of *Gender Gaps* report with selected findings, tables, bibliography, and recommendations for educators and policy-makers. 24 pages/1998.
$6.95 AAUW members/$7.95 nonmembers.

Separated by Sex: A Critical Look at Single-Sex Education for Girls

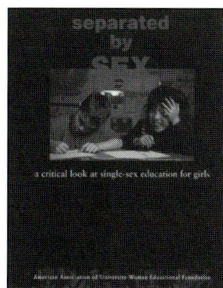

The foremost educational scholars on single-sex education in grades K-12 compare findings on whether girls learn better apart from boys. The report, including a literature review and a summary of a forum convened by the AAUW Educational Foundation, challenges the popular idea that single-sex education is better for girls than coeducation. 102 pages/1998.
$11.95 AAUW members/$12.95 nonmembers.

Gender and Race on the Campus and in the School: Beyond Affirmative Action Symposium Proceedings

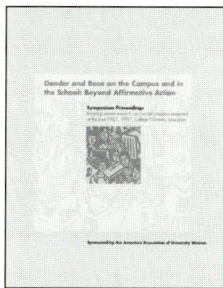

A compilation of papers presented at AAUW's 1997 college/university symposium. Topics include K-12 curricula and student achievement, positive gender and race awareness in elementary and secondary school, campus climate and multiculturalism, higher education student retention and success, and the nexus of race and gender in higher education curricula and classrooms. 428 pages/1997.
$19.95 AAUW members/$21.95 nonmembers.

Girls in the Middle: Working to Succeed in School

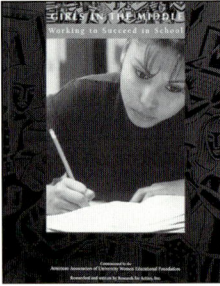

Engaging study of middle school girls and the strategies they use to meet the challenges of adolescence. Report links girls' success to school reforms like team teaching and cooperative learning, especially where these are used to address gender issues. 116 pages/1996.
$12.95 AAUW members/$14.95 nonmembers.

Growing Smart: What's Working for Girls in School—Executive Summary and Action Guide

Illustrated summary of academic report identifying themes and approaches that promote girls' achievement and healthy development. Based on review of more than 500 studies and reports. Includes action strategies, program resource list, and firsthand accounts of some program participants. 48 pages/1995.
$10.95 AAUW members/$12.95 nonmembers.

How Schools Shortchange Girls: The AAUW Report

A startling examination of how K-12 girls are disadvantaged in America's public schools. Includes recommendations for educators and policy-makers as well as concrete strategies for change. 224 pages/ Marlowe, 1995.
$11.95 AAUW members/$12.95 nonmembers.

Hostile Hallways: The AAUW Survey on Sexual Harassment in America's Schools

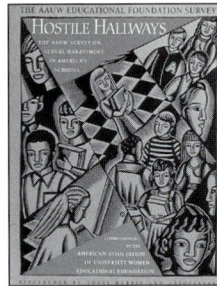

The first national study of sexual harassment in public school, based on the experiences of 1,632 students in grades eight through 11. Report includes gender and ethnic/ racial data breakdowns. Conducted by Louis Harris and Associates. 28 pages/1993.
$8.95 AAUW members/$11.95 nonmembers.

SchoolGirls: Young Women, Self-Esteem, and the Confidence Gap

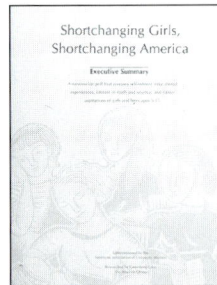

Riveting book by journalist Peggy Orenstein in association with AAUW shows how girls in two racially and economically diverse California communities suffer the painful plunge in self-esteem documented in *Shortchanging Girls, Shortchanging America*. 384 pages/Doubleday, 1994.
$11.95 AAUW members/$12.95 nonmembers.

Shortchanging Girls, Shortchanging America: Executive Summary

Summary of the 1991 poll that assesses self-esteem, educational experiences, and career aspirations of girls and boys ages 9 through 15. Revised edition reviews poll's impact, offers action strategies, and highlights survey results with charts and graphs. 20 pages/1994.
$8.95 AAUW members/$11.95 nonmembers.